P9-ASJ-264

08/24
STRAND PRICE
$ 5.00

BOOK OF
LANDSCAPE GARDENING

AMERICAN SOCIETY OF LANDSCAPE ARCHITECTS
CENTENNIAL REPRINT SERIES

ASLA CENTENNIAL REPRINT SERIES

Country Life: A Handbook of Agriculture and Book of Landscape Gardening (1866)
Robert Morris Copeland

Landscape Architecture, as Applied to the Wants of the West (1873)
H. W. S. Cleveland

Charles Eliot, Landscape Architect (1902)
Charles W. Eliot

The Art of Landscape Architecture (1915)
Samuel Parsons Jr.

Prairie Spirit in Landscape Gardening (1915)
Wilhelm Miller

Landscape-Gardening (1920)
O. C. Simonds

The Spirit of the Garden (1923)
Martha Brookes Hutcheson

Book of Landscape Gardening (1926)
Frank A. Waugh

New Towns for Old (1927)
John Nolen

Landscape for Living (1950)
Garrett Eckbo

The series is underwritten by the Viburnum Foundation.

BOOK OF LANDSCAPE GARDENING

FRANK A. WAUGH

Introduction by
LINDA FLINT McCLELLAND

University of Massachusetts Press / Amherst

in association with

Library of American Landscape History / Amherst

This volume is reprinted from the 1926 edition of
Book of Landscape Gardening by Frank A. Waugh, published by
Orange Judd Publishing Co., Inc.

Printed in the United States of America

LC 2007045094
ISBN 978-1-55849-521-0

Printed and bound by Thomson-Shore, Inc.

Library of Congress Cataloging-in-Publication Data

Waugh, F. A. (Frank Albert), 1869-1943.
Book of landscape gardening / Frank A. Waugh ; introduction by Linda Flint McClelland.
p. cm.— (American society of landscape architects centennial reprint series)
Originally published: New York : Orange Judd Pub. Co., 1926.
Includes bibliographical references and index.
ISBN 978-1-55849-521-0 (cloth : alk. paper)
1. Landscape gardening. I. Library of American Landscape History.
II. Title.
SB472.W4 2007
712—dc22

2007045094

All photographs, plans, etchings, and publications are by Frank A. Waugh unless otherwise noted. Citations for Special Collections and University Archives, W.E.B. Du Bois Library, University of Massachusetts Amherst, have been abbreviated as UMass Special Collections.

CONTENTS

PREFACE

The ASLA Centennial Reprint Series comprises a small library of influential historical books about American landscape architecture. The titles were selected by a committee of distinguished historians and practitioners who identified them as classics, important in shaping design, planting, planning, and stewardship practices in the field and still relevant today. Each is reprinted from the original edition and introduced by a new essay that provides historical and contemporary perspective. The project was initiated by the Library of American Landscape History to commemorate the 1999 centennial of the American Society of Landscape Architects and funded by the Viburnum Foundation.

The names and achievements of many early twentieth-century landscape practitioners have become familiar to students of American landscape history, but information about Frank A. Waugh (1869–1943) has been slow to emerge, in part because Waugh's influence came primarily through writing and teaching rather than design. His significance is illuminated here by Linda Flint McClelland, who sees in Waugh's life's work unswerving advocacy for consideration of "the whole outlook," as he put it, "the country landscape with all its hills, valleys, streams, lakes, forests, and cultivated fields—a commodity which . . . is of the very greatest importance to all our civilization."

In Waugh's view, the landscape architect was first and foremost an artist "capable of seeing, feeling, and understanding . . . the beauties of the landscape, and capable, too, of interpreting these beauties to others." In 1902 he founded the department of landscape architecture at Massachusetts Agricultural College (now the University of Massachusetts Amherst), where he taught students to analyze landscape forms by studying Corot and to understand the music of a rushing stream by playing his flute for them beside it. Among the practitioners he trained through these unconventional methods were several who became prominent in the profession: John Noyes, Stephen Hamblin, Earle Draper, A. D. Taylor, John W. Gregg, and Conrad Wirth, the director of the National Park Service from 1951 to 1964.

Despite his romantic ideas about the transformative effects of landscape beauty, Waugh was also a realist, a passionate advocate of land use planning in an era of explosive development. For many years he also served as a consultant to the U.S. Forestry Service, where he advised on the design of roads, campgrounds, headquarter sites, trails, and viewing points. Waugh's 1935 *Landscape Conservation: Planning for the Restoration, Conservation, and Utilization of Wild Lands for Parks and Forests* reflected insights gained through ecological studies he conducted in the late 1920s and was republished as a training manual for the Civilian Conservation Corps.

Like Wilhelm Miller, also born in 1869, Waugh was a prolific and versatile author, publishing on a variety of topics, from pomology to horticulture to forestry to design. As did many of his colleagues (including Miller), Waugh felt a duty to teach new American homeowners how to make their properties orderly and attractive through the application of sound landscape principles. This was the impetus behind his *Book of Landscape Gardening*, first published in 1899, revised in 1912, and expanded in 1926, when Waugh added several photographs, including many he took himself. Among the new images were tree-lined streets in Amherst, the royal palace at Koblenz on the Rhine, new gardens in California, and ancient gardens in Japan.

McClelland's essay traces the changes in the subsequent editions of the book, noting Waugh's shift in emphasis from village improvement toward conservation. Aiming the last edition at the widest possible audience, the landscape architect wove in several inspirational epigraphs, including passages by O. C. Simonds (whose book, *Landscape-Gardening*, published in 1920, covered many of the same topics) and verse by the Chinese poet T'ao Ch'ien. Among the more than three hundred articles, essays, pamphlets, and books that Waugh produced over the course of his richly productive life, *Book of Landscape Gardening* is his most comprehensive statement on the art of landscape architecture. McClelland's introduction provides a thorough overview of this important work as it deftly situates Waugh in the context of his time and the new profession.

Her essay and extensive bibliography—the first published compendium of Waugh's writings—offer critical information about this influential figure.

Robin Karson, Executive Director
Library of American Landscape History
Amherst, Massachusetts

LALH

Library of American Landscape History, Inc., a nonprofit organization, produces books and exhibitions about American landscape history. Its mission is to educate and thereby promote thoughtful stewardship of the land.

Frank A. Waugh. UMass Special Collections.

INTRODUCTION TO THE REPRINT EDITION

by Linda Flint McClelland

Frank A. Waugh (1869–1943) had grown up on the plains, in McPherson, Kansas, the son of homesteaders who were expected to cultivate the earth and grow a forest in return for their land. His family's difficulty in growing trees in a climate plagued by heavy drying winds, lack of rain, and temperature extremes made a lasting impression on Waugh and seems to have stimulated his interest in a career in horticulture. Indeed, in 1895–96, in three issues of *Garden and Forest*, Waugh wrote about the successes and failures of timber culture in his home district of McPherson, drawing attention to the suitability of the Osage orange, black walnut, and cottonwood for western planting. With some authority, he also pointed to the sycamores, Norway maples, and silver maples as the best street trees for the western plains.[1]

After Waugh's move to the richly forested Northeast—Burlington, Vermont, in 1895 and then Amherst, Massachusetts, in 1902, where he remained for the rest of his life—trees became a central, lifelong focus and theme. He soon became a noted pomologist, writing books and articles about peaches, plums, and apples, and he also wrote

"Pine Trees, Cape Cod." *The Landscape Beautiful* (1910).

about roadside trees, trees for farm woodlots and small home grounds, trees that enveloped and screened garden rooms and outdoor theaters, and trees preserved in national and state parks and forests. Throughout his life Waugh's interest in trees would reflect a striking dichotomy between practical, down-to-earth, and scientifically based knowledge and an almost romantic, poetic sense of beauty. In 1905 Waugh told readers of *Country Life in America* how to plant a tree, while five years later he wrote: "A single tree is beautiful in itself—the symmetry of the perfect elm or pine or palm satisfies the eye like the symmetry of a Greek temple."[2] More than twenty years later he would provide instructions for dressing the edge

Tulip Trees, etching, 1942. UMass Special Collections.

of a forest with informal groupings of trees and shrubs that blended into nature's garden.

This poetic sense led Waugh to write admiringly of the beeches in Berlin's Tiergarten, to photograph the dappled rays of sunlight penetrating a deep forest (*BLG*, 48), and to find beauty in a solitary pair of pines fighting for survival on a windswept dune. A heightened awareness of the "landscape spirit" as expressed in trees remained with him, eventually finding its way into the etchings he created in the last eight years of his life—many having as their topic a single tree or cluster of trees. In these images Waugh was able to convey the gentle sway of barren branches, riveted character of aging bark, and elongated shadows of winter; such images evoke an extremely restful and at times almost mystical mood.[3]

To Waugh, trees were "the most indispensable of materials for landscape making," and in the *Book of Landscape Gardening* trees are the first plants to be considered among the gardener's materials and are given the most thorough treatment in the text.[4] They predominate thematically in the photographs that illustrate the third edition, many taken by Waugh himself. What distinguished Waugh's treatment of trees from the handling of the topic in the popular garden writing of his time was an emphasis on landscape design and straightforward, practical advice, often conveyed in relatively few words. "In any save the smallest places the trees form the framework of the plantings," he wrote, noting that selection, placement, and care in growing plants must all be closely attended to or "the whole composition is apt to fall to pieces" (*BLG*, 163).

The *Book of Landscape Gardening*, one of more than twenty books Waugh wrote on a wide variety of subjects (along with more than 300 technical bulletins, reports, pamphlets, and magazine articles), is notable among contemporary titles in landscape architecture for having been issued in three editions over a span of twenty-seven years—the first in 1899 when Waugh was barely thirty, the second, lightly revised, in 1912, and the final one, revised and slightly expanded, in 1926. The publisher, Orange Judd Company, a well-respected house, considered the book a commercial success in the first two editions, which aimed to help students of landscape gardening and horticulture, park managers, estate owners, teachers,

Naturalistic steps up Hagbourne Hill, designed by F. L. Olmsted for Boston's Franklin Park, in the 1912 edition of *Landscape Gardening*. Photograph by George King.

and garden club members. The third edition was even more popular, attracting readers among the swiftly increasing number of new suburban homeowners in the decade following World War I.

To promote good design practices, Waugh emphasizes the art of landscape gardening, and he discusses in separate chapters each of the formal principles that should guide the artist's work: unity, variety, character, propriety, motive (or theme), and finish (good care of individual plants). Following these he describes what were, in his view, the three major styles of this fine art: 1) natural—the Olmstedian style, derived from English landscape and parks, which had come to dominate landscape architecture in America, and regional variations of it such as the so-called prairie style developed by Jens Jensen; 2) formal

Court of Honor at the 1893 World's Columbian Exposition, as illustrated in the 1899 and 1912 editions of *Landscape Gardening.* Photographer unknown.

Formal garden of Emma Dakin in Amherst, Massachusetts. *Formal Design in Landscape Architecture* (1927).

or "architectural"—inspired by the 1893 Columbian Exposition and the work of architect-artist Charles Platt, whose *Italian Gardens* of 1894 spurred many American designers to emulate the great villas and palaces of Europe; and 3) Picturesque—derived from late eighteenth-century English writings about forest scenery and the sublime in nature and, by 1926, equated in Waugh's mind with the symbolic depiction of nature in Japanese landscape gardening. Unity being the first requirement of artistic design, Waugh cautioned readers that the styles should almost never be mixed in a single composition.

The book also contains practical advice on a variety of "general problems" such as street planting, improving farm and school yards, the handling of water in landscape designs, and laying out suburban home grounds. In the final sections it includes plentiful resources on plant materials (many genera of trees, shrubs, perennials, annuals, bulbs, and vines), and it points readers to what Waugh considered the essential books for beginners.

Waugh's annotated list of thirty-two books included some of what he considered the world's greatest literature, including *L'Art des Jardins* (1879) by French landscape architect Edouard André and *Gartengestaltung de Neuzeit* (1906) by German designer Willy Lange (neither was translated into English). Among the most important American writings was the *Introduction to the Study of Landscape Design* by Henry V. Hubbard and Theodora Kimball, which was first published in 1917 and would remain the profession's chief textbook for decades. As for his personal favorites, Waugh praised O. C. Simonds's *Landscape-Gardening* for its "mature views on the main matters," and

The Complete Garden by A. D. Taylor (one of Waugh's first students) for its extensive lists of plants suitable for American gardens of different types and locations (*BLG*, 232).

By the time the third edition appeared, American landscape literature had grown considerably. The American Society of Landscape Architects, which had been organized in 1899, kept pace with this progress by publishing reviews in its quarterly, *Landscape Architecture*, and even funded the reprinting of several old classics, including those by Humphry Repton (edited by John Nolen), Prince Hermann von Pückler-Muskau (edited by Samuel Parsons Jr. and also translated into English), A. J. Downing, and Edward Kemp (the last two edited and revised by Waugh himself)—all of which appeared on Waugh's reading list.

Waugh began to gain a sense of the artistic goals of landscape design as a student in horticulture at Kansas State Agricultural College (now Kansas State University) beginning in 1886. He was fortunate to have as a teacher J. D. Walters, who headed KSAC's Division of Industrial Drawing and Design. Educated in Switzerland, Walters taught Waugh drafting, free-hand drawing, and art history, and introduced him to landscape design through his work, with the help of the St. Louis landscape architect Maximilian Kern, in carrying out a new plan for the Kansas campus.[5]

Waugh continued his studies at KSAC after graduation, and he took his first teaching job in the fall of 1893 at the new agricultural college in Stillwater, Oklahoma (now Oklahoma State University). It is not surprising that the topic of his master's thesis was a preliminary plan for the new and somewhat barren Oklahoma campus. Walters

View of the Campus Pond, c. 1919, at Massachusetts Agricultural College, designed by Waugh. UMass Special Collections. Photographer unknown.

likely introduced Waugh to the writings of Downing, Kemp, and Jacob Weidenmann, and also to *Landscape Gardening* (1891) by Samuel Parsons Jr., the superintendent of New York's Central Park, which became a valuable resource for Waugh's master's project. Waugh's plan reflected the preference of American designers for the natural style and depended in large part on the planting of suitable trees and shrubs, many native to the western plains.[6] Later as a professor at the Massachusetts Agricultural College, Waugh would again become involved in campus planning. Soon after his arrival there, he began to make inquiries about the ill-fated plan that Olmsted & Vaux had prepared for the college in 1866. By 1908, he had acquired copies of the written report from Frederick Law Olmsted Jr. (no graphic plan existed) and began to make use of its suggestions in his own recommendations for future campus growth and improvement.

Olmsted believed that the ideal plan for an agricultural college must relate to 1) the special calling of the farmer; 2) rural household affairs; and 3) the affairs of rural communities. On the last topic, he wrote: "Nearly every farmer gives considerable thought to matters which are not those of his farm . . . but of the community generally, such as the common roads, bridges, schools, meeting houses, grave yards, monuments, libraries, and lyceums."[7] Waugh heeded Olmsted's call for rural outreach, and in 1913 he instituted a program of civic instruction aimed at improving rural villages and the open countryside in Masssachusetts; the program would become a model for agricultural extension services that, funded by the Smith-Lever Act of 1914, were soon offered at land-grant colleges nationwide.

An event which had for the young Waugh (as for many others) a momentous impact was the World's Columbian Exposition at Chicago in 1893, where Olmsted Sr., Daniel H. Burnham, and many architects, artists, and sculptors created the "White City," which included the naturalistic Wooded Island and the formal Court of Honor. Waugh later wrote that "works of greater artistic merit will often be produced hereafter in America, but works of greater influence, never." Of the millions who visited the fair, Waugh suspected that many "went home inspired with new ideas of beautiful things and with a determination to make their own homes more orderly and artistic, their own grounds more beautiful, and to give their home towns and cities something of the grandeur and magnificence of the White City beside Lake Michigan."[8] The first edition of his *Book of Landscape Gardening* six years later must have been partly aimed at those inspired homeowner-designers.

Two years after the exposition, Waugh moved to Vermont to become a professor of horticulture at the College of Agriculture. Soon he was occasionally writing for and no doubt attentively reading the magazine *Garden and Forest* (1888–97), which likely had as great an impact on the burgeoning profession of landscape architecture as the Chicago exposition. The densely packed weekly was "conducted" by Charles Sprague Sargent, head of the Arnold Arboretum in Boston, and edited by William Stiles, an editor at the *New York Tribune* who was considered a penetrating literary stylist and who wrote many of the editorials. Here Waugh read reports of horticultural advances, profiles of outstanding landscapes, and provocative editorial commentary on such timely issues as landscape preservation, management of public parks, and protection of forest preserves. In an 1890 issue he might have seen a comprehensive bibliography of world garden literature by Henry Codman, Olmsted Sr.'s partner and Sargent's nephew. And he would have read frequently about the great parks and palace grounds of Europe, as well as horticultural advances being made at the Royal Botanical Gardens at Kew (England) and other centers of research abroad. Here too Waugh became acquainted with Charles Eliot's thoughts on the preservation of the Waverly Oaks at Belmont, on a metropolitan park system for Boston that in its design would emphasize the region's outstanding natural features and watersheds, and on landscape forestry as a process for restoring natural beauty.

Waugh would also have read in its pages many articles on the art of landscape gardening by the art critic Mariana Griswold Van Rensselaer, later published in *Art Out-of-Doors*. Waugh would use a quotation from her book as his opening epigraph in the *Book of Landscape Gardening*, and it seems clear that she provided him with the vocabulary to discuss gardening as an art. Van Rensselaer's conceptions harmonized with those of Olmsted, as they strongly argued for landscape architecture as a profession. Indeed, more and more as time went on, *Garden and Forest* was aimed at documenting and even defining the profession in concept and detail. As the century came to a close and publication ceased (in 1897), *Garden and Forest* had gone a long way toward shaping that profession.

Van Rensselaer's articles would have resonated strongly with Waugh given his own artistic sensibilities and interest in the fine arts—not only as a landscape designer, but also as a serious photographer, accomplished flutist, and, later in life, a master printmaker. His student Albert D. Taylor said Waugh was blessed "with a brilliant analytical mind, and with outstanding talent as an administrator, teacher, writer, artist, and musician."[9]

By all accounts Waugh's artistry and creativity extended to his teaching—inside the classroom and out. In 1899, Waugh remarked, "I have always conducted my classes on the assumption that, while no student is likely to become a landscape gardener, all are bound to see many of the beautiful pictures in Nature's gallery, and these they ought to understand and enjoy."[10] For many years in Massachusetts he offered the college's only instruction in art appreciation, using great paintings (especially the work of the French landscape artist Corot, of which he owned a set of prints) to inspire a love of landscape and illustrate the universal principles of fine art. Outdoor study was fundamental to Waugh's approach (he once commented that even the study of economics would be greatly humanized if only students could meet the subject in the garden). Exercises in plant identification would dispatch Waugh's students across the campus and into the surrounding hills in search of climbing vines or native asters. For advanced students the campus became an ideal laboratory where, under Waugh's tutelage, they examined real-life problems and were given the opportunity to execute their own designs.

Waugh's best-known exercise, "landscape links," led students through a series of outdoor viewpoints—a process he compared to an afternoon walk where "one tramps leisurely from point to point, stopping to contemplate at ease each good view."[11] To compare landscape art with the fine art of music, he would encourage his students to listen to the music of a free-flowing stream, and, seated on a ledge-like boulder, he would play his flute in cadence with the sound of "water running downhill." Such lessons were memorable and appealed to nonprofessional as well as professional students.

Among the important elements in the wide network that *Garden and Forest* brought together were the nation's land-grant colleges and their agricultural experiment stations, which were geared toward the practical and often economically productive aspects of agriculture. This became the professional context for Waugh's career as he

"Flute and Brook Harmonize in a Duet," self-portrait published in *American Forests and Forestry Life,* June 1925. UMass Special Collections.

moved eastward, from Kansas and Oklahoma to Vermont, and then to Massachusetts. His horticultural professors in Kansas were correspondents for the magazine, and the greenhouse superintendent was a regular contributor. Seventeen of Waugh's own earliest pieces, on subjects as varied as native plums, timber culture in Kansas, orchid-flowering cannas, and the islands of Lake Champlain, were written for *Garden and Forest.* Waugh, in an 1897 letter to the editor, even assumed the persona of a bicyclist and expressed outrage at the billboards that marred the beauty of country roads—an opinion he shared with Stiles, the editor.[12] This piece foreshadowed his later advocacy for rural improvements and landscape protection. Waugh seemed to announce with those varied pieces the remarkable breadth of interest that remained one of the distinctive hallmarks of his very productive life.

In addition to the land-grant community, many readers of *Garden and Forest* belonged to state horticultural societies, which were often founded by well-connected and scientifically knowledgeable people. Waugh presented his earliest ideas about landscape gardening in a lecture to the Vermont Horticultural Society—which quickly became an article in *The Country Gentleman* in 1898 and was expanded to become the *Book of Landscape Gardening* a year later.[13] A decade later, Waugh similarly presented a study on American practice and practitioners at a meeting of the long-standing Massachusetts Horticultural Society, where it seems he became acquainted with Boston's preeminent landscape architects, Frederick Law Olmsted Jr. and Warren Manning.

Portrait of Liberty Hyde Bailey. UMass Special Collections.

With his move to Vermont in 1895 and his early writing for *Garden and Forest*, Waugh was beginning to vigorously extend his connections within the domains of horticulture, landscape gardening, and publishing. During this early period he traveled to Ithaca, New York, to study briefly at Cornell with Liberty Hyde Bailey, the leading horticulturist in America, who was at the time assembling his comprehensive, multivolume *Cyclopedia of American Horticulture*. (For the 1906 edition Waugh wrote entries on beets, plums, carrots, cucumbers, lilies, salad plants, and "horticulture in Vermont.") Waugh found in Bailey not only a rich source of knowledge but a deeply sympathetic spirit who loved nature, greatly revered the American farmer, and was an admirable model as a scientist and mentor. He later wrote that not only his own career but the entire field of nonprofessional landscape education were "inscribed" with Bailey's name and "freshened by [his] touch."[14] In each edition of the *Book of Landscape Gardening* Waugh used Bailey's words from the book *Garden-Making* (1898) as an epigraph to his own chapter on unity: "Every yard should be a picture . . . with every feature contributing its part to one strong and homogeneous effect" (*BLG*, 11).

Bailey's encouragement of Waugh's writing and his high opinion of Waugh's scientific acumen instilled great confidence in the younger man and led him to explore new avenues in journalism. In 1898 he became horticultural editor for *The Country Gentleman*, one of the nation's oldest weeklies devoted to agriculture and rural life, a position he held for thirteen years. In the meantime he wrote as well for *Country Life in America*, initially edited by Bailey, and several other magazines.

The connection with Bailey introduced Waugh to other interesting and powerful people who would further enrich his life and work—for example, the publisher Frank Doubleday and his wife Nellie, who both wrote about gardening (she under the pseudonym Neltje Blanchan). Doubleday published *Country Life in America* and in 1905 introduced *Garden Magazine*, whose first issue carried an article on foxgloves written by Waugh and another

"A German Iris," in the first issue of *The Garden Magazine*, February 1905.

on irises written by Blanchan and illustrated with photographs by Waugh. In 1909 Blanchan wrote the lively and informative *American Flower Garden*, known for its striking photographs taken by pioneers in horticultural photography such as J. Horace McFarland.

Probably through Bailey, Waugh met McFarland, one

Portrait of Robert Frost. UMass Special Collections.

of the most effective figures of the Progressive Era. McFarland operated a printing business with extraordinary capabilities—particularly his pioneering methods of photographic engraving with color. Waugh's own artistry in photography seems to have been sharpened by his association with McFarland, who encouraged his ventures into the genre of America's Photo-Secession movement (he emulated the work of Gertrude Kasebier, Frank Eugene, and Edward Steichen) and portraiture (he photographed famous individuals including Robert Frost and President William Howard Taft). Not only was McFarland's press used by Doubleday and the Macmillan Company

(Bailey's publisher), but McFarland was a zealous advocate of the City Beautiful movement and the preservation of outstanding American scenery.

As president of the American Civic Association, which was founded in 1904 (Waugh was a member), McFarland was highly successful in marshaling professional support for the promotion of urban parks, civic planning, and scenery preservation, and he ignited a grassroots movement that provided popular support for civic improvements across the nation. McFarland supported the clean-up and restoration of Niagara Falls, and, along with John Muir and John Burroughs, he battled passionately but unsuccessfully against the building of a dam in the Hetch Hetchy Valley of Yosemite National Park.

Waugh took on many of McFarland's causes. In fact, during the Yosemite crisis, Waugh and McFarland corresponded often, and later when McFarland asked Waugh's advice on the ablest landscape architect to help spearhead the joint ACA and ASLA campaign to establish a national park service, Waugh suggested two—Olmsted Jr., and Manning.[15] McFarland was well acquainted with Manning, who under McFarland's supervision had designed the waterfront park and improvements for McFarland's home town, Harrisburg, Pennsylvania. The ACA president, however, selected Olmsted, in large part due to his leadership on the McMillan Commission for the design of the nation's capital and the firm's established reputation in landscape preservation, which dated to the late 1860s, when the elder Olmsted, who chaired the Yosemite Board of Commissioners, wrote the pivotal report leading to the creation of the first Yosemite park by the State of California.

Also important was Waugh's friendship with Wilhelm Miller, who was Bailey's assistant editor on the *Cyclopedia* and became the editor of Doubleday's *Garden Magazine* (beautifully printed by McFarland's company). Miller would go on to write several important books, including one about the midwestern landscape architecture of Jens Jensen and O. C. Simonds, *Prairie Spirit in Landscape Gardening* (1915, rpt. 2003 by LALH). Miller became well known for his advocacy of native plants and disapproval of exotics, which he adamantly argued for in *The "Illinois Way" of Beautifying the Farm* (1914). Waugh admired Miller's *What England Can Teach Us about Gardening* (1911), praising it as "a book of dashing criticism illuminating many of our American problems" (*BLG*, 231). Miller enlisted Waugh for the first issue of *Garden Magazine.* With his piece "All the Foxgloves Worth Cultivating," Waugh reached a knowledgeable set of readers who had keen interests in particular plant genera—members of gardening societies who considered themselves amateur horticulturists and landscape designers. This was a somewhat new audience for Waugh, and Miller clearly appreciated Waugh's versatility as a writer and photographer.[16]

Waugh and Miller corresponded for many years, sharing a common interest in preserving the native character of the rural countryside, particularly in the early years of the agricultural extension movement when Miller, working for the University of Illinois, drew attention to what he called the "prairie spirit" of midwestern landscape design and

View of Wilder Hall, ca. 1919, showing Waugh's choice of a hillside setting overlooking the campus pond and landscape design with shrubbery and vines. UMass Special Collections. Photographer unknown.

became an advocate of the use of native plants on farms, private estates, roadsides, and public parks. Characteristic of Miller was his advice in the epigraph for the chapter on hardy perennials that "those effects which grow naturally out of the soil and out of true economy will be recognized as the most artistic" (*BLG*, 187).

Early in the century Waugh also became friendly with Jensen, whose naturalistic work creating idealized landscapes with native plantings and landforms evocative of the plains deeply impressed him. He and Jensen became regular correspondents, and it soon became obvious that Waugh had real sympathy for Jensen's view that American designers "study our own conditions and develop something that harmonizes with our climate and our people."[17]

After seven years in Vermont, Waugh moved with his family to Amherst in 1902, where he immediately established and became head of the Department of Landscape Gardening at Massachusetts Agricultural College (now University of Massachusetts Amherst). The first such program in the United States had started at Harvard just two years before, and Waugh's, designed as a four-year curriculum, began admitting students in 1903. At the end of the decade Waugh wrote a piece called "Ten of My Boys," about graduates of the program and their thriving careers in the new profession of landscape architecture.[18] He was very attentive to his students' employment prospects, and he helped place them in good situations, including the offices of the Olmsted Brothers, Jens Jensen, Warren Manning, and John Nolen.

A measure of Waugh's influence over the years was the quality of his students and the scope of their work. They included John Noyes, who for many years was the chief landscape architect at the Missouri Botanical Garden in St. Louis; Stephen Hamblin, who worked for Warren Manning, taught at Harvard, and was director of the botanical garden there; Conrad Wirth—son of the Minneapolis park superintendent Theodore Wirth—who became director of the National Park Service in the 1950s, after directing the training and work of President Franklin D. Roosevelt's Civilian Conservation Corps in the national and state parks two decades earlier; Earle Draper, who, after working for John Nolen, developed over three hundred subdivisions, campuses, cemeteries, estates, and parks; John W. Gregg, who headed the landscape gardening and floriculture program at the University of California in Berkeley and who invited Waugh west to teach a summer course in 1924 and introduced him to the outstanding formal landscape work in Mediterranean styles then burgeoning in California—an experience that influenced his writing of the *Formal Design in Landscape Architecture* in 1927; and Albert D. Taylor, one of the first MAC graduates, who by the late 1920s had offices in Cleveland and Florida and employed a dozen or more landscape architects, some of them also Waugh's students. In his 1943 tribute to Waugh in *Landscape Architecture*, Taylor wrote: "No single individual has done more to inspire the layman to live a richer life by bringing to his home surroundings the orderly and attractive elements of landscape architecture."[19]

Of all Waugh's students perhaps Hamblin most closely expressed his teacher's ideas about landscape gardening and art. By the mid 1920s Hamblin was emerging as an authority on the expressive use of plants in landscape design and an early proponent of an ecological approach to planting. Writing in a 1924 issue of the ASLA quarterly, *Landscape Architecture*, he drew attention to the artistry of planting that could be observed in the work of well-known landscape architects, and urged readers to study such work in great detail. Hamblin offered advice on "a study of ecology to be used in art," and wrote, "Much that nature does we can adopt wholly or adapt to the requirements of civilization. Then in each wood and field we can suggest plants to be added, to continue the work of the genius of nature, or bring in the feeling of the presence of humanity."[20]

Hamblin's words identify a central theme that emerged in Waugh's work during the second and third decades of the twentieth century as his focus shifted from horticulture to, first, a concern about the declining state of rural America and, second, a strong advocacy for the preservation of the natural beauty and richness of American wilderness. Waugh directed his writings to describing how damaged park and forest land should be restored, how beautiful natural landscapes could be preserved and at the same time be made accessible for public pleasure, and how planting should be done ecologically so as to recreate nature as sympathetically as possible.

In 1980, Conrad Wirth recalled his teacher. "[He] went into depth on the relationship between man and the natural environment. He . . . believed that man-made landscape developments, to be successful, must meet the needs of the people and that the natural elements were a part of these needs. [He] proceeded on the principle that man's advanced culture and social development required certain modern conveniences but that these utilities should not be ugly or destructive of the needed natural environment."[21]

In Waugh's first decade at MAC he wrote extensively about horticultural subjects in particular, publishing books with Orange Judd on apple orchards, plum growing, fruit harvesting and marketing, and systematic pomology. In 1902 he was a founder of the Society for Horticultural Science along with Liberty Hyde Bailey. Waugh also wrote many pieces for experimental station bulletins. In 1908 he undertook a survey of past and practicing American landscape

"An Old Orchard of Northern Spy." *The American Apple Orchard* (1908).

architects, the results of which he published in *The Country Gentleman* and *Park and Cemetery*. In 1910 his illustrated book *The Landscape Beautiful* (also published by Orange Judd) contained much of this material in the form of essays based on his lectures and classroom exercises.[22]

The same year he traveled to Europe for seven months. During this period he wrote twenty-four pieces for *The Country Gentleman*, sometimes sending several for a single issue. He wrote—characteristically—about a wide variety of subjects: roses, apples, a butter boycott, urban woodlands, horticultural education, street markets, music, and the labor problem. While in Berlin he studied at the Royal Horticultural School with the landscape architect Willy Lange, whose writings had caught his attention several years earlier, perhaps at the suggestion of Jens Jensen. Lange's work fascinated Waugh, who

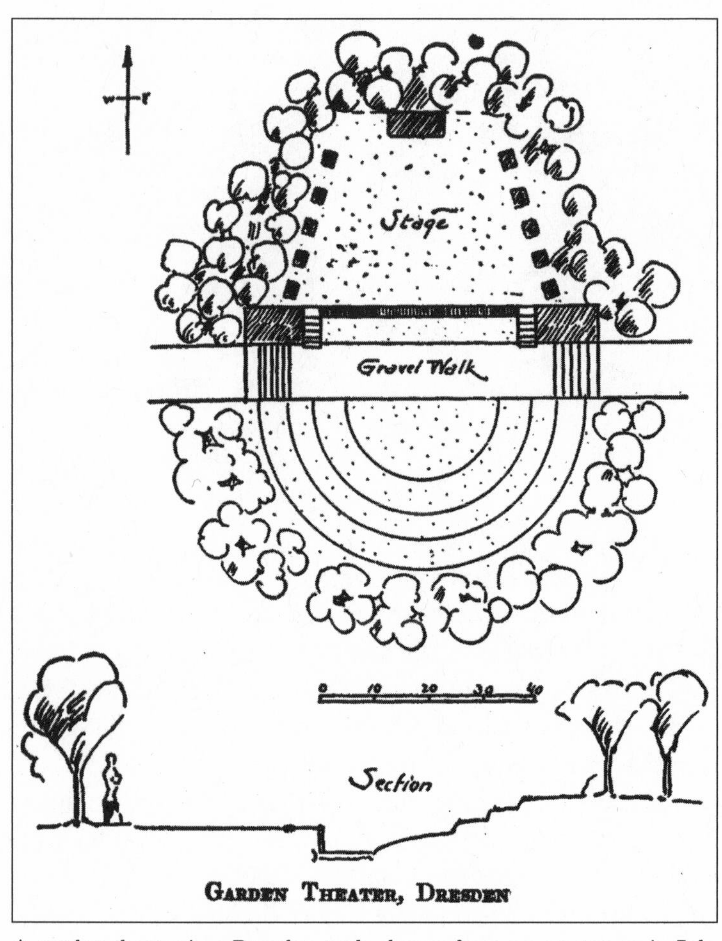

A garden theater in a Dresden park, drawn from a pace survey in July 1910. *Outdoor Theaters* (1917).

described the German landscape architect as one who "wants his gardens running over full of flowers" and for whom "design is a thoroughly subordinate matter." Lange's love of nature, horticultural knowledge, and ecological approach to landscape design would profoundly influence Waugh for many years to come. Waugh simply explained Lange's ecological method as one where "plants should be assembled in a garden in their natural relationships together with one another in nature, placing such a plant society in its proper soil and on its proper geologic formation."[23]

An important outcome of his study of Lange and other naturalistic designers was the 1917 book *The Natural Style of Landscape Gardening*. Though the book was criticized by his peers for its references to the "landscape spirit," for Waugh, who advocated an empirical approach to design that involved close study of natural forms, it was the designer's ability to "clarify and interpret the spirit of the place" that distinguished the work of a true artist.[24] Waugh adopted Lange's ideas about motive (which he once called Lange's "hobby") as a principle of artistic design. He introduced the concept in his book on the natural style, thus laying the groundwork for a new chapter that described the brook and pine tree motives in some detail and appeared in the final edition of the *Book of Landscape Gardening*. In the mid-1920s, Waugh began engaging his students in projects that applied Lange's ecological method to American conditions. These studies—on topics such as running water, the ecology of the roadside, and physiography of lakes and ponds—are considered by many to be Waugh's greatest contributions to twentieth-century landscape architecture.

Waugh maintained his European connections, and years later he was invited by the German writer Marie Luise Gothein to contribute to her two-volume *History of Garden Art*, which then as now was considered a standard reference work. The first two editions, in 1914 and 1924, were written in German, but when the third edition appeared in 1928 it was translated into English for the first time and included a new section, "Landscape Architecture in North America," written by Waugh.[25] This was a personal and professional triumph for Waugh, signifying not only his role as one of the chief chroniclers of the field, but also international recognition for the accomplishments of America's practitioners—past and present.

The years after he returned from Germany marked two new directions in Waugh's work, each running parallel to and reinforcing the other. Both were logical outgrowths of his interest in the art of developing and protecting beautiful landscapes. First was his involvement in what he called "country planning," and second was his consulting for the United States Forest Service on landscape engineering and planning in national forests. Both emerged from a sense of the landscape being irrevocably altered and, in some cases, lost altogether. Waugh regretted the disappearance of, for example, the bluestem grasses and sage on the plains and their replacement with corn and wheat; the loss of one of the most beautiful valleys in Yosemite to support the growth of metropolitan San Francisco; the loss of great forests to slash-and-burn timber cutting; and the disorderly precipitous growth of cities. For him these were all interconnected.

Waugh returned home from Germany to find support growing for rural improvement—not only as a result of the findings of the Commission on Country Life chaired by Bailey, but also as a special interest of MAC's president, Kenyon Butterfield, who was an acclaimed rural economist, had served on the commission, and was eager to encourage the college's work in this direction. In 1913 Waugh hired P. H. Elwood Jr., a graduate of Bailey's program, as the college's first instructor of civic improvement. Together they examined all the elements of rural communities—roads, schools, farms, cross-roads, rail stations, village centers, parks, and playgrounds—and they collaborated on a number of technical bulletins aimed at farmers and community leaders. Many of these were also published in *American City*, one of the first journals devoted to planning in the United States. In 1914 Waugh published *Rural Improvement*, his first book on the topic, which drew on his and Elwood's experience as well as his own observations on country planning in Canada and Germany.

Waugh's efforts remained overshadowed by city planning, which had emerged as its own discipline in the first two decades of the twentieth century. He did, however, win the support of the ACA, McFarland's organization, which published his early pamphlet *Country Planning* in 1915, and Bailey, who in addition to chairing President Theodore Roosevelt's Country Life Commission in 1908 paid highest tribute to the American farmer in his book *The Holy Earth* (1915). Waugh even convinced the editors of *American City* to issue a special "town and country" edition each month for several years, and he garnered the support of the Russell Sage Foundation in setting up a clearinghouse to promote country planning and sponsoring a conference devoted to the topic at MAC in the early 1920s.

Waugh became more and more concerned about the inevitability of change and its physical effect on rural communities and the open countryside, and in 1924 he published a full-length book, *Country Planning*, in which he attempted to set out planning principles that could be applied systematically and rationally to the problems of the country. He insisted that city planning as it was developing—indeed regional planning too—virtually ignored the country, producing decisions that benefited the city only, and he wrote with notable vigor that the physical problems of the country were largely matters of public property that had to be addressed with public money, expertise, and time. Aiming at an audience of farmers, homeowners, and community leaders, Waugh wrote: "Changes are being constantly made. Farms are sold, subdivided or consolidated. New land is opened up and settled. New roads are built. . . . New schoolhouses have to be built, new county buildings provided, even new parks, forests and playgrounds. . . . Since changes must come, since some are much better than others, and since they all involve expenditures of money, it is much the best to foresee them and plan for them. Planning for such inevitable changes in the country is country planning. And that's all there is to it."[26]

Waugh's thinking quickly transcended his formative

ideas about rural improvements and the "landscape beautiful," and he began to address the highly politicized issues of land use. His concern for land use went far beyond the preservation of notable scenic and historic features and by the mid-1930s extended into the national dialogue about the utilization of natural resources. To a large extent Waugh was a pioneer in land-use planning; in this he joined O. C. Simonds, Benton MacKaye, and Warren Manning (who wrote passionately about these issues in his 1919 National Plan).

The disturbing trends Waugh saw in 1924 were not reversed; thirteen years later in "Physical Aspects of Country Planning" he railed again at city planning: "The country, if considered at all, is regarded merely as that area where the city gets its food, water, and exercise. Grand parkways are projected through miles of rural landscape, beginning at one city and ending in another. . . . Does the city want a bath? The engineers go out into the country and make a new reservoir, condemning another 50 or 100 square miles of territory for the purpose, dispossessing the farmers, extinguishing country villages, and even obliterating the cemeteries. The forefathers, trying to get a little quiet sleep, are peremptorily exhumed and carted off to the official dump." Waugh's response here was triggered by the bitter conflict that arose close to home between big city interests and rural communities over plans to dam the Swift River and create a huge reservoir in the hills east of Amherst. The project would provide abundant water for metropolitan Boston but sacrifice five country villages (which meant also relocating the village cemeteries). Waugh's focus on land use continued: "Our original land subdivision seems to have been based on the idea that all forests were to be extinguished and all land converted into farms. We now know that this was a tragic mistake." In this article he examined the disappearance of back-country roads in favor of highways and greater speed. Such slow roads, Waugh believed, were of great importance for keeping travelers truly in touch with rural life and beautiful landscape. He ended the piece thus: "Finally there is ever to be considered the whole outlook—the country landscape with all its hills, valleys, streams, lakes, forests, and cultivated fields—a commodity which, as I firmly hold, is of the very greatest importance to all our civilization. Cities, libraries, picture galleries might be destroyed and built again, but if we lose the landscape we lose our own souls completely and irrevocably."[27]

The principles behind country planning were similar to those that informed Waugh's work with the national forests for nearly twenty years. Of particular relevance was his understanding of the natural style of landscape design, which was based on natural forms and as much as possible used native plants. Visually, Waugh described the natural style as "unsymmetrical, not obviously balanced, not apparently enclosed and not marked by visible boundaries."[28] Furthermore he developed ecological ideas about natural plant communities, and natural conditions of growth such as soil, drainage, and climate, that were of key importance in guiding landscape architects in the parks and forests, especially where restoration of land or water was needed and mass plantings desirable. The art

"Sugar Loaf Mountain—A Massachusetts State Park." *Textbook of Landscape Gardening* (1922).

of grouping trees was another measure fundamental to the natural style, and he realized that for most cases a group of five or more was most appropriate and most reflective of plant communities in nature. For Waugh the landscape work in the national forests and parks, which would accelerate in the 1930s with the establishment of the Civilian Conservation Corps, offered the natural style "the greatest opportunities offered to any art at any time in the world's history."[29]

In this work he had an immediate impact on larger policies. Between 1917 and 1936, Waugh spent many summers consulting for the United States Forest Service, making recommendations on the design of roads, campgrounds, headquarters sites, trails, and outstanding viewpoints and vistas within the national forests—what in 1918 he called "landscape engineering." In the early years he developed a plan for Grand Canyon Village (when it was still a national forest); later he would travel to the forests of Colorado, Utah, California, the Southern Appalachians, and Oregon, and in 1930 he served on a prestigious three-member panel (with Olmsted Jr. and John Merriam of the Carnegie Institution) to advise Congress on recreational planning for the Mount Hood National Forest.

While ASLA and ACA were campaigning for the establishment of a National Park Service, Waugh began to envision the national park concept in a much broader context—one that extended from national forests and parks to national monuments, state parks and forests, local reservations, and even the public highway. He saw the designation of landscape reservations at various levels of government as one of the most important developments in the history of American landscape architecture—one that distinguished American design from its European precedents. Equally great, however, was his concern that the American public be aware of the nation's rich legacy of landscape reservations, and find in them pleasure and recreation. In the *Scientific Monthly* in 1918 he wrote:

"Through a considerable effort the public is slowly becoming conscious of their physical magnificence, their wide extent, their unsurpassed scenery, their overpowering grandeur. Still there is little popular appreciation of the significance of the national park idea itself. Nothing like this system of recreation grounds was ever established in any country in the world before, nor was there ever any similar undertaking of such tremendous reach, such high human possibilities."[30] To Waugh a sound national park policy entailed centralized oversight for the entire domain of American parks—national parks and forests, state parks and forests, reservations held in private trust, county and rural parks, and parkways—regardless of who administered or managed these lands.

In the 1930s, as the Great Depression deepened, Conrad Wirth, who had become an assistant director of the National Park Service heading up the Civilian Conservation Corps efforts in state parks, asked Waugh to write a technical manual that would be a compilation of his ideas on recreation in the parks and forests, and would cover land reclamation, development of lakes, and the creation of trails and campgrounds. Wirth's idea was to get good technical information and clear discussion of basic principles to the CCC camps and the many landscape architects who supervised the work in both national and state parks and forests throughout the country. First issued in 1935 in typescript, the manual was called *Landscape Conservation: Planning for the Restoration, Conservation, and Utilization of Wild Lands for Parks and Forests*. In great detail the manual treated trail placement and grading; view points and vistas; the use of bonfires and outdoor theaters (two subjects of special interest to Waugh); shaping tree plantations to harmonize with the natural surroundings; preservation of physiographic features such as rock formations and sand dunes; re-creating vegetation around developed lakes in natural concentric zones; and assuring that landscape architects had a complete knowledge of the vegetation in any given park or forest before they began to work.[31]

Landscape Conservation was an outgrowth of Waugh's work for the national forests, his earlier thinking on the natural style, and ecological studies he conducted with his students in the late 1920s and had published in *Landscape Architecture* several years before.[32] It was serialized in *Parks and Recreation*, the journal of the organization of park superintendents, and in 1937 it was republished as a training manual for the CCC organization aimed at preparing enrollees for future careers in park design as well as for their day-to-day fieldwork.

The preservation of America's scenic wonders and native landscape was a twofold effort—requiring the professional skills of the landscape architect and the heartfelt advocacy of an educated and appreciative public. In 1922, Waugh had written: "The professional landscape architect should be first of all an artist, capable of seeing, feeling, and understanding . . . the beauties of the landscape, and capable, too, of interpreting these beauties to others."[33] In the chapter on landscape reservations, which first appeared in the 1926 edition of the *Book of Landscape Gardening*, Waugh describes what he sees as the "layman's" duty to understand and enjoy the "glorious landscape preserved . . . in these noble parks and forests." He wrote, "As one sees more and more of the best landscapes one's appreciation grows. . . . Our duty and our privilege are to see what is good and enjoy it." This Waugh believed was one of the great "benefits imparted by landscape gardening" (pp. 157–59).

Though Frank Waugh did not join the ASLA until long after its establishment (serving then as head of the committee on landscape extension work), and though he was a practitioner only in a limited sense, he was during most of his life deeply engaged in the issues facing professional practitioners. He became friends with many of them, worked with them, found work for his students in their offices, and prepared a number of students for graduate studies at Cornell or Harvard. He obviously knew the universe of landscape architects as well as anyone in America. His contributions to the field, through his students, through his voluminous writings especially on art, the natural style, and the formal style, and through the country planning and park and forest work, are a good deal more substantial and lasting than is commonly recognized. Modern environmental thinkers would find in him an astute ally.

One wonders about Waugh's persistence in using the term "landscape gardening" long after the profession in the United States became known as "landscape architecture." In 1899, when the *Book of Landscape Gardening* first appeared, Waugh defended the term on the basis that it was associated with the English gardening tradition and called attention "to the lowlier problems" which were of greatest concern to the general public and for which an understanding of artistic principles was most needed. Later editions resounded with Waugh's concern for the common landscape and echoed his early dictum: "All persons ought to endeavor to understand the methods and aims of landscape art, as they endeavor to master the alphabet of literature."[34]

Waugh remained convinced that "landscape gardening" was the domain of the average American and certainly an appropriate title for a book intended as "a simple introduction to the simplest principles which rule in the realm of our art, and which indeed rule in a large part of our lives" (*BLG*, x). Although he claims in the 1926 edition that both terms—along with "landscape engineering" and "landscape design"—are interchangeable, he clearly uses "landscape architecture" only in references to the profession and its practitioners, as is apparent in the preface and the chapter on landscape reservations.

Gradually Waugh would come to accept the term he had criticized for being "too long," having "too large a sound," and suggesting "princely and magnificent undertakings" (*BLG*, 5). In fact, the year before the final edition appeared, he wrote in an article, "American Ideals in Landscape Architecture," in *Landscape Architecture* that the passage of twenty-five years since the ASLA's founding made it possible to define a "steadily clarified vision of ideals" at least as far as professional practice was concerned.[35] About this time he also changed the name of his department from "landscape gardening" to "landscape architecture." When Waugh's treatise on the formal style appeared in 1927, the intended title, *The Formal Garden in America* (*BLG*, 223), had become *Formal Design in Landscape Architecture*.

In Waugh's mind the distinction between the needs of the average homeowner and those of the professional practitioner had become more apparent as the profession took form and expanded in the early decades of the twentieth century. In an attempt to make "timely additions without destroying the freshness of a youthful book" (p. ix), Waugh orchestrated a number of changes while maintaining most of the original text. The changes to the *Book of Landscape Gardening* offer some closing insights into his thinking and the far-reaching nature of his life and career.

The most dramatic change in the 1926 edition is Waugh's choice of new photographs, many of which he had taken himself. Through these photographs, readers join Waugh and his neighbors in their modest but comfortable home grounds and gardens, and they enter Waugh's universe—a college campus that conveys a dignified rural aesthetic, tree-lined streets that evoke a village ideal, and places near and far (Japan, England, Germany, California, the Midwest, and the Berkshire hills) where he at some time in his life sought inspiration and intellectual satisfaction.[36] These include a view of the Kürfurstliches Schloss, the royal palace at Koblenz on the Rhine (which first appeared in the 1912 edition), recalling the great influence that Waugh's 1910 sabbatical to Germany had on his own education and career (p. 88). The images depicting the gardens of Japan do not appear to be Waugh's own; instead they seem to anticipate his deepening interest in the cultures of Japan and China—places he would visit in the 1930s and depict in several of the etchings he produced in his later years.

Also noteworthy are the images of Waugh's own work on the MAC campus in Amherst. Primarily executed in the natural style, these designs included the campus pond shown through a tracery of sumac and cut-leaved maple (p. 119), his greatly prized rhododendron garden in full flower (p. 182), and the open lawns with foreground trees that provided a dignified and naturalistic setting for the Alumni Memorial Building, which was built in 1922 as both war memorial and student union (p. 62).

Whereas earlier editions depicted the great works at Versailles, Olmsted and Vaux's Central and Prospect Parks, Jensen's Humboldt and Garfield Parks, and the famous Italian garden at H. H. Hunnewell's estate in Wellesley, Massachusetts, the 1926 edition purposefully avoids naming the places illustrated in the text, giving at most a regional or national affiliation. Only a handful can be recognized as the work of well-known designers; these include what appears to be the Rubens Estate in Glencoe, Illinois, by Jens Jensen (p. 100); the sunken Italian garden at Brookside, in Great Barrington, Massachusetts, by Ferruccio Vitale (p. 78); the grounds and gardens designed by the renowned sculptor Daniel Chester French for Chesterwood, his summer home in Stockbridge, Massachusetts (pp. 16 and 116); and Spring Grove Cemetery (p. 54) in Cincinnati, laid out by the German-trained

Entrance to garden designed by Daniel Chester French for his studio at Chesterwood in Stockbridge, Massachusetts. *Formal Design in Landscape Architecture* (1927).

landscape architect Adolph Strauch, whose "lawn method" greatly influenced Waugh, as it did O. C. Simonds, enabling them to reconcile the formality of classical architecture with the naturalistic landscape—be it a cemetery or a college campus.

Also striking are the new epigraphs Waugh weaves into the text—one from Simonds's *Landscape-Gardening* (1920) praising the beauty of "undulating" fields where "the grown crop waves in the wind" (*BLG*, 132); another expressing the sentiment of a twentieth-century British poet tracing the song of a nightingale "from lawn to lawn down terraces of sound" (p. 113). And not at all surprising is the German text by Willy Lange which exalts the tumultuous and evocative power of water in its wildest and most elemental, primeval forms (p. 118).

Frank and Alice Waugh in their home garden on the campus of Massachusetts Agricultural College. *Formal Design in Landscape Architecture* (1927).

Finally, as a fitting closing to the book, we find the autobiographical verse of Chinese poet T'ao Ch'ien (from the Period of Six Dynasties), who, having retired to his beloved country home, his plowing done and his seeds sown, once more finds himself content to sit and read (p. 227). Some readers may wonder if Waugh is alluding here to his own approaching retirement, but with almost twenty-five years of managing the landscape and horticultural programs at MAC behind him and thirteen years ahead before mandatory retirement, his career was far from over. The publication of the *Book of Landscape Gardening* in 1926 did, however, mark a turning point in that career as his interests shifted from the American home and village toward the conservation of natural areas through the blending of artistic principles and ecological methods. The impact of

Vine-laden farmhouse "by the side of the road," the Waugh family home on the grounds of Massachusetts Agricultural College. UMass Special Collections. Photographer unknown.

Professor Waugh cultivating his vegetable garden. *Textbook of Landscape Gardening* (1922).

the changes to the final edition, bringing it away from an illustrated lecture series and more toward a book suitable for a homeowner's fireside reading, is large indeed—undoubtedly a true measure of Waugh's strong beliefs that "the fundamental principles on which landscape architecture rests do not change" and that the power to improve the American landscape and to preserve what is already beautiful must be given to ordinary people.

NOTES

1. Frank A. Waugh, "Some Notes on Timber-culture," *Garden and Forest* 8 (18 December 1895): 502–3; "Trees of Minor Importance for Western Planting—I," *G&F* 9 (15 January 1896): 23; and "II," *G&F* 9 (29 January 1896): 42–43.

2. Waugh, "How to Plant a Tree," *Country Life in America* 7 (January 1905): 303. Quotation comes from Frank A. Waugh, "Ministry of Trees," in *Landscape Beautiful* (New York: Orange Judd, 1910), 35.

3. Waugh's etchings were featured in an exhibition at the University of Massachusetts Central Gallery in Amherst in 2003. They may be viewed online at http://people.umass.edu/abischof/frankwaugh/waugh_exhibit.html.

4. Waugh, "Ministry of Trees," 32.

5. Richard Longstreth, "From Farm to Campus: Planning, Politics, and the Agricultural College Idea in Kansas," *Winterthur Portfolio* 20, no. 2/3 (Summer/Autumn 1985): 170–74.

6. Waugh, "A Preliminary Study of the Grounds of the Oklahoma Agricultural and Mechanical College and Experiment Station," Master's thesis, Kansas State Agricultural College, Manhattan, 1894, Special Collections and Archives, W. E. B. Du Bois Library, University of Massachusetts, Amherst.

7. Frederick Law Olmsted, Olmsted, Vaux & Co., *Preliminary Report upon a Plan for the General Arrangement of the Premises of the Massachusetts Agricultural College* (Amherst: Trustees of the Massachusetts Agricultural College, 1866), 13–14. Olmsted and Vaux's report was also published as Olmsted, *A Few Things to Be Thought of before Proceeding to Plan Buildings for the National Agricultural Colleges* (New York: American News Company, 1866).

8. Waugh, "On American Masterpieces in Landscape Architecture," in *Landscape Beautiful*, 187–88. For Waugh the Chicago exposition was of personal significance: his horticulture professor E. A. Popenoe from KSAC worked on the horticultural exhibits, and his classmate Albert Dickens, to whom he later dedicated the *Book of Landscape Gardening*—"He also loves the plains"—worked on the Kansas state exhibit. Dickens went on to head the expansion of KSAC's horticultural department in the first three decades of the twentieth century and became Kansas's first state forester.

9. A. D. Taylor, "Frank Albert Waugh: A Biographical Minute," *Landscape Architecture* 34, no. 1 (October 1943): 26.

10. F. A. Waugh, "Preface," in *Landscape Gardening* (1899, rpt., New York: Orange Judd, 1906), iii. Note that the first and second editions of Waugh's book were named *Landscape Gardening.*

11. Frank A. Waugh, "The Landscape Links," in *Textbook of Landscape Gardening Designed Especially for the Use of Non-professional Students* (New York: John Wiley & Sons, and London: Chapman & Hall, 1922), 295.

12. "Protection for a Public Interest," *G&F* 9 (8 April 1896): 149.

13. Unsigned, "The Fine Art of Gardening," *Country Gentleman* 63 (21 July 1898): 568.

14. Waugh, *Textbook of Landscape Gardening*, v.

15. Ernest Morrison, *J. Horace McFarland: A Thorn for Beauty* (Harrisburg, Pa.: Historical and Museum Commission, 1995), 175.

16. "All the Foxgloves Worth Cultivating," *Garden Magazine* 1 (January 1905): 15, 90.

17. Jens Jensen, "An Imposing Exhibit of German Garden Art," *Park & Cemetery* 18, no. 4 (June 1908): 346–47.

18. Waugh, "Ten of My Boys," *Suburban Life* 8 (June 1909): 329–30. Although the names are fictitious, he was clearly referring to former students Charles H. Halligan, John W. Gregg, Arthur Peck, and Albert D. Taylor.

19. Taylor, "Waugh, A Biographical Minute," 26.

20. Stephen F. Hamblin, "The Mental Planning of Planting," *LA* 14, no. 2 (January 1924): 94.

21. Conrad L. Wirth, *Power, Politics, and the People* (Norman: University of Oklahoma Press, 1980), 11.

22. [Unsigned], "Our Landscape Architects: Their Qualities and Defects," *CG* 73 (30 April 1908): 442; Waugh, "American Landscape Architects and Their Work," *Park and Cemetery* 18, no. 6 (August 1908): 383–84; "A Survey of American Landscape Architecture—Part I," *P&C* 19, no. 9 (November 1909): 155–57; "Part II," *P&C* 19, no. 10 (December 1909): 179–80; Waugh, "On American Landscape Gardening," in *Landscape Beautiful*, 111–34, also "On American Landscape Gardeners," 149–76, and "On American Masterpieces of Landscape Architecture," 177–202.

23. F. A. Waugh, "German Landscape Gardening," *CG* 75 (25 August 1910): 790. Waugh found Lange's work similar to that of Warren Manning in the United States.

24. Waugh, *The Natural Style of Landscape Gardening* (Boston: Richard G. Badger, 1917), 24. See also Melanie L. Simo, *Forest & Garden: Traces of Wildness in a Modernizing Land* (Charlottesville: University Press of Virginia, 2003), 218–19.

25. "Landscape Architecture in North America, United States and Canada: Historical and Critical Survey," in *A History of Garden Art*, ed. Marie Luise Gothein, 3rd ed. (New York: Dutton, 1928).

26. Frank A. Waugh, *Country Planning: An Outline of Principles and Methods* (New York: Harcourt, Brace & Company, 1924), 3–4.

27. Frank A. Waugh, "Physical Aspects of Country Planning," *Journal of Land and Public Utility Economics* 13 (August 1937): 232–35; online at http://jstor.org/view/15489000/sp040051/04x1151g/O.

28. Waugh, *Natural Style*, 20.

29. Ibid., 144–45.

30. "A National Park Policy," *Scientific Monthly* 6, no. 4 (April 1918): 305.

31. Linda Flint McClelland, *Building the National Parks: Historic Landscape Design and Construction* (Baltimore: The Johns Hopkins University Press, 1998), 443–50.

32. F. A. Waugh, "Ecology of the Roadside," *LA* 21, no. 2 (January 1931): 81–92; "Natural Plant Groups," *LA* 21, no. 3 (April 1931): 169–79; "The Physiography of Lakes and Ponds," *LA* 22, no. 2 (January 1932): 89–99.

33. Waugh, *Textbook of Landscape Gardening*, 276.

34. Waugh, "Preface," in *Landscape Gardening* (1899), iv.

35. Waugh, "American Ideals in Landscape Architecture," *LA* 15, no. 3 (April 1925): 151.

36. Most of these depict Waugh's own garden—sometimes with family members—and those of his Amherst neighbors and associates (pp. 6, 20, 40, 114, 125, and 192). Several clearly stem from his 1924 visit to Southern California (frontispiece and pp. 111,127, 166), a family trip to Nashville (p. 130), and a 1925 trip to England (p. 56).

SELECTED LIST OF PUBLICATIONS

The following bibliography includes most of the published works that are attributed to Waugh under his own name or, in some cases, a pseudonym. Many additional articles and notes are believed to have appeared in *Country Gentleman* during the years he served as horticultural editor. In addition, he published a number of entries in the *Florists' Exchange*, which are not included here. A versatile writer, Waugh often reworked his material for different audiences; sometimes these were professional planners, landscape architects, amateur photographers, and educators, and often the gardening public as well.

Unless otherwise noted, Waugh's writings were signed as F. A. Waugh or Frank A. Waugh. In general, he used the initialized form for his scientific and agricultural writings and his full name for his work relating to landscape design, planning, conservation, gardening, and photography.

ABBREVIATIONS

AmC	*American City*
CG	*Country Gentleman*
CLA	*Country Life in America*
GM	*Garden Magazine*
G&F	*Garden and Forest*
GM&HB	*Garden Magazine and Home Builder*
LA	*Landscape Architecture*

MACAESB	*Massachusetts Agricultural College Agricultural Extension Service Bulletin*, Amherst, Mass.
MACAESC	*Massachusetts Agricultural College Agricultural Extension Service Circular*, Amherst, Mass.
MAESB	*Massachusetts Agricultural Experiment Station Bulletin*, Amherst, Mass.
MAESR	*Massachusetts Agricultural Experiment Station Report*, Amherst, Mass.
OAESB	*Oklahoma Agricultural Experiment Station Bulletin*, Stillwater, Okla.
P&R	*Parks and Recreation*
WHC	*Woman's Home Companion*
VAESB	*Vermont Agricultural Experiment Station Bulletin*, Burlington, Vt.

1893–1894

Test of Varieties of Vegetables. OAESB no. 9 (1893/94).

Press Bulletin Excerpts. OAESB no. 11 (1894).

Grapes. OAESB no. 14. (1894).

1895

Garden Vegetables. OAESB no. 15 (1895).

"What Is a Cantaloup?" *G&F* 8, no. 376 (8 May 1895): 183–84.

"The Munson Grape Trellis." *G&F* 8, no. 376 (8 May 1895): 186.

"Some Notes on Timber Culture." *G&F* 8 (18 December 1895): 502–3.

1896

"The Pollination of Plums." *VAESB* no. 53 (1896): 43–64.

Houseplants and How to Grow Them. Rutland, Vt.: A. W. Perkins Co., 1896.

"Trees of Minor Importance for Western Planting—I." *G&F* 9, no. 412 (15 January 1896): 23; "II." *G&F* 9, no. 414 (29 January 1896): 42–43.

"Protection for a Public Interest." *G&F* 9, no. 424 (8 April 1896): 149.
"Some Causes Which Affect Productiveness." *Kansas Farmer* (30 July 1896).
"Salad Plants and Plant Salads." *VAESB* no. 54 (November 1896): 68–79.
Apple Growing in Grand Isle County. VAESB no. 55 (December 1896).

1897

"Hardy Apples for Cold Climates." *VAESB* no. 61 (1897): 21–32.
"Definiteness of Variation and Its Significance in Taxonomy." *Botanical Gazette* 25, no. 3 (March 1897): 193–95.
"College Instruction in Horticulture." *G&F* 10, no. 471 (3 March 1897): 89.
"The Islands of Lake Champlain." *G&F* 10, no. 472 (10 March 1897): 93.
"Plum Trees for Ornamental Planting." *G&F* 10, no. 480 (5 May 1897): 177–78.
"Cannas, America." *G&F* 10, no. 480 (5 May 1897): 178.
"Maple Sugar in Vermont." *G&F* 10, no. 480 (5 May 1897): 179.
"Some Phases of Weed Evolution: Excerpts." *Science* 5 (21 May 1897): 789–91.
"New View of the Hortulana Plums." *G&F* 10, no. 497 (1 September 1897): 340–41.
"Wayland Group of Plums." *G&F* 10, no. 498 (9 September 1897): 350.
"Lilium Henryi." *G&F* 10, no. 499 (15 September 1897): 365.
"Cheney Plum." *G&F* 10, no. 499 (15 September 1897): 367.
"Notes on the Orchid-flowering Cannas." *G&F* 10, no. 501 (29 September 1897): 384–85.
"More Orchid-flowering Cannas." *G&F* 10, no. 512 (15 December 1897): 496.
"Enzymic Ferments in Plant Physiology." *Science* 6 (24 December 1897): 950–52.

1898

Notes on Horticultural Nomenclature: Some Suggestions for the Nurseryman, Fruit Grower, Gardener, Seed Grower, Plant Breeder and Student of Horticulture. New York: American Gardening, 1898.

"The Vegetable Garden." *Garden-Making: Suggestions for the Utilizing of Home Grounds*, Garden-Craft Series, edited by L. H. Bailey. 1898; reprint, New York: Macmillan, 1905. 353–85.

"Home-grown Grapes in Vermont." *VAESB* no. 62 (1898): 37–44.

"Hybridization: With Special Reference to the Horticulture of North America." *American Gardening* 19 (1898).

Hybrid Plums. VAESB no. 67 (1898).

"Studies in Nomenclature—I: General Problems." *CG* 63 (9 June 1898): 448. "II: Pomological Rules." *CG* 63 (16 June 1898): 468. "III: The Names of Garden Vegetables." *CG* 63 (23 June 1898): 488. "IV: Examples of Scientific Methods." *CG* 63 (7 July 1898): 508. "V: Property Rights in Name." *CG* 63 (7 July 1898): 528.

[unsigned]. "The Fine Art of Gardening." *CG* 63, no. 2373 (21 July 1898): 568.

"A New Pomological Code." *CG* 63, no. 2387 (27 October 1898): 848.

1899

Landscape Gardening: Treatise on the General Principles Governing Outdoor Art; With Sundry Suggestions for Their Applications in the Commoner Problems of Gardening. New York: Orange Judd, 1899.

"The Home Fruit Garden." *VAESB* no. 74 (1899): 90–97.

"Conspectus of Genus Lilium." *Botanical Gazette* 27, no. 5 (May 1899): 235–54.

1900

"Checklist of Hybrid Plums." *VAESB* no. 75 (1900): 102–110.

"Report of the Horticulturist." *13th Annual Report of the Vermont Experiment Station* (26 November 1900).

"Apples of the Fameuse Type." *VAESB* no. 83 (December 1900): 84–92.

1901

Plums and Plum Culture: A Monograph of the Plums Cultivated and Indigenous in North America, with a Complete Account of Their Propagation, Cultivation and Utilization. New York: Orange Judd, 1901.

Fruit Harvesting, Storing, Marketing: A Practical Guide to the Picking, Sorting, Packing, Storing, Shipping and Marketing of Fruit. New York: Orange Judd, 1901.

"Plum Culture." *VAESB* no. 89 (1901): 20–28.

F. A. Waugh and M. B. Cummings. *Apple Growing in Addison County. VAESB* no. 90 (1901): 32–36.

"Gum-Bichromate Printing." *The Photo-Miniature* 2, no. 22 (January 1901): 399–40.

"Landscape Photography." *The Photo-Miniature* 3, no. 25 (April 1901): 1–36.

1903

Systematic Pomology: Treating of Description, Nomenclature and Classification of Fruits. New York: Orange Judd, 1903.

"Report of the Horticulturist." *15th Annual Report of the Vermont Experiment Station, 1901–1902.* Burlington, Vt., 1903. 249–67.

"Our Agricultural Advance." *50th Annual Report of the Secretary of the Massachusetts State Board of Agriculture, 1902.* Boston, 1903. 85–100.

"Fruits for the Home Garden: Varieties and Culture." *Massachusetts Board of Agriculture Bulletin* (1903): 29–39.

1904

Frank A. Waugh, George E. Stone, and Henry T. Fernald. *Fungicides, Insecticides, Spraying Calendar. MAESB* no. 96 (May 1904).

A Farm Woodlot. MAESB no. 97 (May 1904).

The Graft Union. MAC Technical Bulletin no. 2 (October 1904).

1905

Packing and Marketing Fruits. St. Joseph, Mo: The Fruit-Grower Company, 1905.

Success with Stone Fruits. St. Louis, Mo.: The Fruit-Grower Company, 1905.

"Harvesting and Marketing Apples." *52nd Annual Report of the Secretary of the Massachusetts State Board of Agriculture.* Boston, 1905. 386–95.

"How to Plant a Tree." *CLA* 7 (January 1905): 303.

"Suggestive Tree Lists and Planting Estimates." *CLA* 7 (January 1905): 303.

"All the Foxgloves Worth Cultivating." *GM* 1 (February 1905): 15, 90.

"Dwarf Fruit Trees." *Transactions of the Massachusetts Horticultural Society*, part 1 (11 February 1905): 47–56.

"Some Recent and Important Changes in the Business of Fruit Growing." *2nd Annual Report of the Vermont State Horticultural Society* (9 February 1905): 70–77.

"Art of Lawn Making." *GM* 1 (March 1905): 78.

"Improvements That Don't Improve." *CG* 70 (4 May 1905): 427.

"Best Plums for Special Places and Purposes." *CLA* 8 (July 1905): 352.

"Complicated Art of Plum Growing." *CLA* 8 (July 1905): 330–31.

"Unsophisticated Zinnias." *Country Calendar* 1 (July 1905): 268.

"Protecting Fruit Trees in Winter." *Country Calendar* 1 (November 1905): 676, 678–79.

1906

Dwarf Fruit Trees: Their Propagation, Pruning and General Management, Adapted to the United States and Canada. New York: Orange Judd, 1906.

"School Gardens as a Preparation for College." *Report of Committee on School Gardens and Native Plants.* Boston: Massachusetts Horticultural Society, 1906. 10–11.

"Beet." *Cyclopedia of American Horticulture*, ed. L. H. Bailey, vol. 1. New York: Macmillan, 1906. 140–41.

"Carrot." *Cyclopedia of American Horticulture*, ed. L. H. Bailey, vol. 2. New York: Macmillan, 1906. 254.

"Cucumber." *Cyclopedia of American Horticulture*, ed. L. H. Bailey, vol. 2. New York: Macmillan, 1906. 405–7.

"Lilium." *Cyclopedia of American Horticulture*, ed. L. H. Bailey, vol. 3. New York: Macmillan, 1906. 914, 916–23.

"Plum." *Cyclopedia of American Horticulture*, ed. L. H. Bailey, vol. 5. New York: Macmillan, 1906. 1373–75.

"Salad Plants." *Cyclopedia of American Horticulture*, ed. L. H. Bailey, vol. 5. New York: Macmillan, 1906. 1598.

"Horticulture in Vermont." *Cyclopedia of American Horticulture*, ed. L. H. Bailey, vol. 6. New York: Macmillan, 1906. 1917–18.

[unsigned], "The Massachusetts College." *CG* 71 (4 January 1906): 12.

"The Progress of Horticulture." *CG* 71 (4 January 1906): 26–27.

"Stimulants for Seeds." *CG* 71 (18 January 1906): 66.

"Dwarf Fruit Trees for Suburban Gardens." *CLA* 9 (March 1906): 564–66.

[unsigned]. "Annuals for the Home Grounds." *CG* 71 (24 April 1906): 402.

[unsigned]. "Arbor Day Suggestions." *CG* 71 (8 May 1906): 426.

[unsigned]. "The Care of a Lawn." *CG* 71 (10 May 1906): 450.

[unsigned]. "Planning the Home Grounds." *CG* 71 (17 May 1906): 474.

[unsigned]. "Plant Breeding." *CG* 71 (24 May 1906): 522.

1907

"Peach Culture." *54th Annual Report of the Secretary of the Massachusetts State Board of Agriculture, 1906.* Boston, 1907. 446–56.

"Variation in Peas." *MAESR* no. 20 (1907): 65–70.

1908

The American Apple Orchard: A Sketch of the Practice of Apple Growing in North America at the Beginning of the Twentieth Century. New York: Orange Judd, 1908.

"Plum Culture in Massachusetts." *55th Annual Report of the Secretary of the Massachusetts State Board of Agriculture, 1907.* Boston, 1908. 355–61.

"Notes on the Propagation of Apples." *MAESR* no. 20 (January 1908): 61–64.

F. A. Waugh and C. S. Pomeroy. "The Physiological Constant for the Germinating Stage of Cress." *MAESR* no. 20 (January 1908): 71–80.

F. A. Waugh and C. S. Pomeroy. "Variation in Peas." *MAESR* no. 20 (January 1908): 171–76.

[unsigned]. "Our Landscape Architects: Their Qualities and Defects." *CG* 73 (30 April 1908): 442.

"American Landscape Architects and Their Work." *Park and Cemetery* 18, no. 6 (August 1908): 383–84.
"The Western Farmer's Advantages." *CG* 73 (10 September 1908): 861.
"Some Agricultural Contrasts: The East and the West." *CG* 73 (17 September 1908): 885.
"Strawberry Culture." *Massachusetts Crop Report* (Boston, October 1908): 30–39.

1909

"Strawberry Culture in Massachusetts." *56th Annual Report of the Secretary of the Massachusetts State Board of Agriculture, 1908*. Boston, 1909. 415–22.
F. A. Waugh and J. Shaw. "Plant Breeding Studies in Peas." *MAESR* no. 22, part 1 (1909): 168–75.
F. A. Waugh and J. Shaw. "Variation in Peas." *MAESR* no. 21, part 2 (January 1909): 167–73.
"The Influence of Stock on Cion in the Graftage of Plums." *MAESR* no. 21, part 2 (January 1909): 174–82.
"Ten of My Boys." *Suburban Life* 8 (June 1909): 329–30.
"A Survey of American Landscape Architecture—Part I." *Park and Cemetery* 19, no. 9 (November 1909): 155–57. "Part II." *Park and Cemetery* 19, no. 10 (December 1909): 179–80.

1910

The Landscape Beautiful: A Study of the Utility of the Natural Landscape, Its Relation to Human Life and Happiness, with the Application of These Principles in Landscape Gardening, and in Art in General. New York: Orange Judd, 1910.
"Trees for Beauty and Comfort." *WHC* 37 (March 1910): 9.

"The Farmer Abroad." *CG* 75 (17 March 1910): 278.

"The Meat Question—An American Farmer Abroad." *CG* 75 (24 March 1910): 300.

"Farmer's Week in Berlin—An American Farmer Abroad." *CG* 75 (24 March 1910): 291. "Farmer's Week in Berlin, II—An American Farmer Abroad." *CG* 75 (31 March 1910): 318–19.

"Birthday of Queen Louise." *CG* 75 (7 April 1910): 348.

"The Berlin Apple Supply." *CG* 75 (14 April 1910): 374.

"Spring in Germany." *CG* 75 (5 May 1910): 446–47.

"German Butter Boycott." *CG* 75 (5 May 1910): 450.

"Royal Botanical Garden." *CG* 75 (12 May 1910): 470–71.

"A German on Our Fruit Trade." *CG* 75 (19 May 1910): 494.

"The Cost of Fruit Growing as Practiced in Germany." *CG* 75 (26 May 1910): 518.

"Fruit Blossoms of Werder." *CG* 75 (2 June 1910): 543.

"German Plum Trees and Currants." *CG* 75 (9 June 1910): 565.

"A Great City Woodland." *CG* 75 (9 June 1910): 572.

"Old Friend in Europe: Stringfellow and Mulch System." *CG* 75 (16 June 1910): 584.

"A Horticultural School." *CG* 75 (23 June 1910): 604.

"Street Markets in Germany." *CG* 75 (30 June 1910): 632.

"Milk and Its Products in Berlin." *CG* 75 (7 July 1910): 649.

"In a German Rose Garden." *CG* 75 (21 July 1910): 684.

"Dwarf Fruit Trees." *CG* 75 (28 July 1910): 704.

"Music in Berlin." *CG* 75 (28 July 1910): 712.

"Farm Land in Europe." *CG* 75 (25 August 1910): 786.

"German Landscape Gardening." *CG* 75 (25 August 1910): 790.

"The Labor Problem." *CG* 75 (15 September 1910): 860.

1911

Frank A. Waugh, ed. *Kemp's Landscape Gardening: How to Lay Out a Garden, 4th Edition: Revised and Adapted to North America.* New York: John Wiley and Sons, 1911.

"My Tree Friends in Winter." *WHC* 38 (February 1911): 16.

"Cookery as a Sport for Men." *Century* 81 (April 1911): 955–58.

"Small Home Fruit Garden." *WHC* 38 (September 1911): 13.

1912

Beginner's Guide to Fruit Growing: A Simple Statement of the Elementary Practices of Propagation. New York: Orange Judd, 1912.

Landscape Gardening: Treatise on the General Principles Governing Outdoor Art; With Sundry Suggestions for Their Application in the Commoner Problems of Gardening. 2nd ed. New York: Orange Judd, 1912.

"Farmers' Calendar." *The (Old) Farmer's Almanack 1913*, ed. Robert B. Thomas. No. 121. Boston: William Ware and Co., 1912. 6–29.

"Rough-Housing." *Independent and Weekly Review* 72 (25 January 1912): 183–84.

"Short-Order Gardens." *WHC* 39 (February 1912): 25.

"Garden of Perennials." *WHC* 39 (March 1912): 25.

"Garden of Hardy Shrubs." *WHC* 39 (April 1912): 19.

"The Versatile Plum." *CG* 77 (27 April 1912): 17.

"People's Picture Galleries: American Parks." *WHC* 39 (May 1912): 48–49.

"Civic Improvement." *The Commonweal* 1, no. 3 (May 1912): 8–11.

"Friendly Summer Trees." *WHC* 39 (July 1912): 8.

Civic Improvement in Village and Country. MACAES, *Facts for Farmers* 2, no. 12 (August 1912).

"Glorious Dutch Bulbs." *WHC* 39 (September 1912): 14.

"Indian Summer in the Garden." *WHC* 39 (October 1912): 185.

"The Important Rural Question: The Problem of Marketing." *Business America* (October 1912): 50–51.

"Winter Resort at Home." *WHC* 39 (November 1912): 17.

1913

The American Peach Orchard: A Sketch of the Practice of Peach Growing in North America at the Beginning of the Twentieth Century. New York: Orange Judd, 1913.

"The Little Town Beautiful: Ways and Means of Organizing Civic Improvement in Rural Communities." *CG* 78, no. 1 (4 January 1913): 5, 32.

"The Opportunity of the Country Village." *AmC* 8 (January 1913): 43–45.

"Home Vegetable Garden." *WHC* 40 (March 1913): 16.

[F. Biehler, pseud.]. "Lovely Garden Lilies." *WHC* 40 (March 1913): 42.

"A Concrete Case of Village Improvement." *AmC* 8 (2 March 1913): 281–82.

"Chickens in the Back-Yard." *WHC* 40 (April 1913): 10.

[F. Biehler, pseud.]. "Loveliest Shrub of the Garden." *WHC* 40 (April 1913): 29.

"First Aid in the Garden." *WHC* 40 (May 1913): 8.

"Flowers in Nature's Garden." *WHC* 40 (June 1913): 17.

[F. Biehler, pseud.]. "June Days in the Garden." *WHC* 40 (June 1913): 30.

"Spirit of the Garden." *WHC* 40 (July 1913): 9.

"Housekeeping with Plants." *WHC* 40 (October 1913): 16.

[F. Biehler, pseud.]. "Winter's Store: Keeping Fruits and Garden Vegetables." *WHC* 40 (December 1913): 34.

1914

Rural Improvement: The Principles of Civic Art Applied to Rural Conditions, including Village Improvement and the Betterment of Open Country. New York: Orange Judd, 1914.

F. A. Waugh and P. H. Elwood Jr. *Country School Grounds*. *MACAESC* no. 32 (1914).

"Finding Happiness in Winter's Garden." *WHC* 41 (January 1914): 9.

[Robert Lane Wells, pseud.] "Alderbrook Farm." *WHC* 42 (February 1915): 21; (March 1915): 26; (April 1915): 25; (May 1915): 36; (June 1915): 22; (July 1915): 21; (August 1915): 21; (September 1915): 24; (October 1915): 27; (November 1915): 25; (December 1915): 27; and 43 (January 1916): 24.

"Fun of Garden Planning." *WHC* 41 (February 1914): 35–38.

"How to Sell Apples: Practical Advice in Regard to Marketing." *Boston Evening Transcript*, 28 February 1914.

[F. Biehler, pseud.]. "Soils and Fertilizers." *WHC* 41 (March 1914): 37.

[F. Biehler, pseud.]. "Sweet Sweet-pea." *WHC* 41 (March 1914): 36.

"Guarding the Garden: Questions of Hedges, Screens and Climbers." *WHC* 41 (April 1914): 5.

[F. Biehler, pseud.]. "Kitchen Garden." *WHC* 41 (April 1914): 39.

"A New Garden Motif." *Suburban Life* 18 (April 1914): 245.

F. A. Waugh and P. H. Elwood Jr. *Street and Roadside Planting*. MACAES, *Facts for Farmers* 4, no. 9 (May 1914).

"Making and Maintaining a Hedge." *GM* 19 (June 1914): 287–89.

"Queen of the Garden." *WHC* 41 (July 1914): 13.

"Country Roads and Their Benefits." *CG* 79 (July 1914): 18.

"Lived-in Garden." *WHC* 41 (August 1914): 24–25.

"From a Country Window." *CLA* 26 (August 1914): 54.

[F. Biehler, pseud.]. "Good Old-Fashioned Peony." *WHC* 41 (September 1914): 35.

[F. Biehler, pseud.]. "Frost Proof Garden." *WHC* 41 (October 1914): 31.

"Joys of Fishless Fishing in Streams and Elsewhere." *Countryside* 19 (October 1914): 185.

"A. J. Downing: Pioneer Landscape Architect." *Park and Cemetery* 24, no. 9 (November 1914): 296–97.

"The Arts of Peace." *The Penn State Farmer* 7 (November 1914): 213–17.

1915

"Making the Garden Habitable." *Gardener's Chronicle of America* 19, no. 3 (March 1915): 107–10.

[F. Biehler, pseud.]. "Fern Garden." *WHC* 42 (April 1915): 31.

"Rural Railway Station Grounds." *AmC* 12 (May 1915): 378–80.

"Country Planning—The Country Has as Much Right to Be Planned as the City." *AmC* 13, Town and Country ed. (July 1915): 14–15.

"Country Woman's Opportunities." *WHC* 42 (July 1915): 18.

"Study for a Rural Neighborhood Center." *AmC* 13, Town and Country ed. (September 1915): 186–89.

"What to Do for Bridgeville." *House Beautiful* 38 (October 1915): supplement, xxx–xxxi, xxxiv–xxxv, xxxviii.

"Discovering a Part of America." *Countryside Magazine* 21 (December 1915): 302–3.

1916

The Agricultural College: A Study in Organization and Management and Especially in Problems of Teaching. New York: Orange Judd, 1916.

"Horticultural Phases of Civic Art." *Standard Cyclopedia of Horticulture*, ed. L. H. Bailey, vol. 4. New York: Macmillan, 1916. 1811–13.

"Village Improvement in Relation to Planting." *Standard Cyclopedia of Horticulture*, ed. L. H. Bailey, vol. 5. New York: Macmillan, 1916. 2658–60.

Country Planning. The American Civic Association series II, no. 8. Washington, D.C., January 1916.

"The Country Cross-Roads." *AmC* 14, no. 3 (March 1916): 235–36.

[F. Biehler, pseud.]. "Charm of the Pansy." *WHC* 43 (March 1916): 23.

"Six Trees in the Orchard." *Countryside Magazine* 22 (April 1916): 209–10.

[F. Biehler, pseud.]. "Strawberries in the Home Garden." *WHC* 43 (April 1916): 23.

"Medlar." *Countryside Magazine* 22 (April 1916): 259.

[F. Biehler, pseud.]. "Bird Garden." *WHC* 43 (May 1916): 26.

"Landscape Gardening." *Practical Husbandry of Maine* 6, no. 3 (May 1916): 591–93.

F. A. Waugh and P. H. Elwood Jr. *Street and Roadside Planting. Facts for Farmers* 6, no. 5 (MAC: Amherst, January 1916); Massachusetts Agricultural College Agricultural Extension Service Leaflet no. 16 (January 1916); and "Street and Roadside Planting." *AmC* 14 (June 1916): 571–74.

The Town Common. MACAESB no. 7 (June 1916); "Town Common." *AmC* 15, Town and Country ed. (August 1916): 128–32.

"It's the Prettiest Street in Town." *WHC* 43 (July 1916): 11.

"Putting Life into the Garden." *GM* 24 (August 1916): 12–13.

"Some Garden Theaters." *The Architectural Review* 4, no. 9 (September 1916): 161–67.

1917

The Natural Style in Landscape Gardening. Boston: Richard G. Badger, 1917.

Outdoor Theaters: The Design, Construction and Use of Open-Air Auditoriums. Boston: Richard G. Badger, 1917.

Recreation Uses on the National Forests: A Study of Their Extent and Character, with a Discussion of Public Policies and Recommendations as to Methods of Development and Administration. Washington, D.C.: U.S. Department of Agriculture, Forest Service, 1917.

Civic Improvement in Village and Country. MACAESC no. 11 (1917).

"Glimpses into Frostless Gardens." *CLA* 31 (February 1917): 37–40.

"Tree Education—A Talk on Pruning." *Countryside Magazine* 24 (February 1917): 81–82.

"Better Countryside Roads." *Countryside Magazine* 24 (March 1917): 123–34.

"Everyman's Vineyard." *Countryside Magazine* 24 (March 1917): 154.

"Shears in the Shrubbery." *Countryside Magazine* 24 (June 1917): 329.

Review of *The Peaches of New York* by U. P. Hedrick et al. *Science* 46, no. 1192 (2 November 1917): 439–40.

"Wild Lilacs." *Horticulture* 26, no. 19 (10 November 1917): 499.

1918

Landscape Engineering in the National Forests. Washington, D.C.: U.S. Department of Agriculture, Forest Service, 1918.

A Plan for the Development of the Village of Grand Canyon, Arizona. Washington, D.C.: U.S. Department of Agriculture, Forest Service, 1918.

"College Teaching in Agriculture." *School and Society* 7, no. 162 (2 February 1918): 130–32.

"Photographing the Forests." *Photo-Era* 40 (February 1918): 59–63.

"A National Park Policy." *Scientific Monthly* 6, no. 4 (April 1918): 305–18.

"A Camera and a Sporting-Chance." *Photo-Era* 40 (May 1918): 237–39.

"Technical Problems in National Park Development." *Scientific Monthly* 6, no. 6 (June 1918): 560–67.

"Flags for the Garden." *Independent and Weekly Review* 95 (7 September 1918): 320.

1919

"Cold Comfort." *Independent and Weekly Review* 97 (11 January 1919): 58–59.

"Color in Gardens." *WHC* 46 (May 1919): 37.

"Useful Landscape Gardening on the Farm." *The Farmer's Advocate* 54 (11 December 1919): 2218.

1920

"A Sideline of Fruit—How You Make It Pay on Your Farm." *Farm & Fireside* (January 1920): 17–20.

"Ten Best Shrubs." *WHC* 47 (February 1920): 43.

"The Seven Mountains of Massachusetts—Famous Peaks in the State That Have Become Public Reservations." *Springfield Republican*, 1 February 1920.

"Where Shall We Ride Today? Landscape near Springfield Offers Endless Panorama of Fine Views." *Springfield Republican*, 15 April 1920.

"The Technic of Landscape Gardening." *Park and Cemetery* 30, no. 3 (May 1920): 77–79.

"Occupational Therapy in Tuberculosis." *Scientific Monthly* 10 (May 1920): 438–56.

"The Public Road: Our Great National Park." *House Beautiful* 47 (June 1920): 508–9.

Frank A. Waugh, ed. *Reports of Committee on Ten-Year Fruit Program for Massachusetts.* Massachusetts Fruit Growers' Association, Inc. June and December 1920.

"The Opportunity of the Country Village." *House Beautiful* 48 (October 1920): 276–77, 312.

1921

Frank A. Waugh, ed. *Landscape Gardening. Works of Andrew Downing Jackson.* 10th ed. New York: John Wiley & Sons, 1921.

"Ornamental Trees—Some Imported Kinds Are Good, But Our Native Species Head the List." *CG* 86 (1 January 1921): 10.

"Landscape Gardening and Music." *Park International* 2, no. 2 (March 1921): 170–71.

"The Market Price on Landscape." *Outlook* 127 (16 March 1921): 428–29.

"How the Country Town Has Become a Better Place for a Summer Home." *Boston Transcript*, 30 March 1921.

"Native Trees in City Streets." *AmC* 24 (May 1921): 497.

"A Comparison of Town Plans." *LA* 11, no. 4 (July 1921): 161–66.

"Photographic Diversions of a Landscape Architect." *Photo-Era* 47 (July 1921): 26–27.

"Why Is a National Monument?" *Outlook* 129 (28 September 1921): 130–32.

"The Way My Father Farmed in Kansas More Than Forty Years Ago." *Farm & Fireside* 45, no. 10 (October 1921): 4, 14–15.

1922

Textbook of Landscape Gardening, Designed Especially for the Use of Non-Professional Students. New York: John Wiley & Sons, 1922.

"Recreation Problems in District 4 National Forests: Report of a Survey." Manuscript, 1922. U.S. Forest Service.

"Recreation Uses in Forestry." *The Empire Forester* 3, no. 1 (1922): 21–24.

Frank A. Waugh, ed. "Report of a Committee of the National Conference on Instruction in Landscape Architecture." In "Extension Work in Landscape Architecture: A Symposium." *LA* 12, no. 2 (January 1922): 61–65.

"How's Your Capillarity?" *CG* 87 (28 January 1922): 17, 32.

"What Is a Forest?" *Journal of Forestry* 20, no. 3 (March 1922): 209–14.

"How to Plant an Apple Tree." *CG* 87 (1 April 1922): 26.

"How to Prune an Apple Tree." *CG* 87 (8 April 1922): 32.

"Art for All." *School and Society* 15, no. 382 (22 April 1922): 437–41.

"Beyond the Boulevards." *Outlook* 131 (24 May 1922): 147–48.

"Petticoat Hill for Example (A Memorial Park.)" *Outlook* 131 (23 August 1922): 679–80; reprinted in *32nd Annual Report of the Trustees of Public Reservations.*

"Standardized World." *School and Society* 16 (4 November 1922): 527–29.

1923

"The Whole Philosophy of Transplanting—It's Against Nature's Methods, But It Gets Results." *CG* 88 (13 January 1923): 6, 32.

"If I Had an Apple Tree—These Are the Easy Things I'd Do to Make It a Model Producer." *CG* 88 (3 February 1923): 5, 32.

"Humanistic Technology." *School and Society* 17, no. 428 (10 March 1923): 274–75.

"How to Escape the Movies." *Outlook* 134 (23 March 1923): 30.

Review of *Gartenbilder* by Willy Lange. *LA* 13, no. 3 (April 1923): 218.

"An Oasis Called Hurricane—A 1923 American Model Is This Dry-land Beauty Spot in Utah." *CG* 88 (12 May 1923): 7.

"Canoeist's Tripod." *Outlook* 134 (24 May 1923): 257.

"Recreation in the National Forests." *National Municipal Review* 12, no. 6 (June 1923): 295–98.

"Spiritual Biography." *Survey Midmonthly* 50 (1 July 1923): 383–85.

"The Town Planning Board." *LA* 14, no. 1 (October 1923): 38–42.

"Photographing for Lantern Slides." *Photo-Era* 51, no. 4 (October 1923): 190–93.

"Conservation ad Absurdum." *Scientific Monthly* 17, no. 5 (November 1923): 498–505.

1924

Country Planning: An Outline of Principles and Methods. The Farmer's Bookshelf Series, ed. Kenyon L. Butterfield. New York: Harcourt, Brace and Company, 1924.

"Wealth of Forests." *The North American Review* 219 (January 1924): 59–64.

"Children Should Go to Church." *Outlook* 136 (12 March 1924): 445.

"Frontiering." *Survey Midmonthly* 52 (1 June 1924): 290–92.

"A Simple Outdoor Theater." *LA* 14, no. 4 (July 1924): 253–56.

Portrait. *House and Garden* 46 (September 1924): 98.

Country Planning: A Selected Bibliography. Bulletin of the Russell Sage Foundation Library, no. 67. Forest Hills, N.Y., October 1924.

"Personal View of California Gardens." *GM&HB* 40 (December 1924): 233–35.

1925

"American Ideals in Landscape Architecture." *LA* 15, no. 3 (April 1925): 151–54.

"Water Running Down Hill." *American Forests and Forestry Life* 31 (June 1925): 352–53.

"Town Meeting." *Survey Midmonthly* 54 (1 July 1925): 389.

"Nantucket Gardens." *GM&HB* 41 (August 1925): 465–67.

"Notes on English War Memorials." *LA* 16, no. 1 (October 1925): 6–14.

"Where-fore Country Planning." *AmC* 33 (November 1925): 514–16.

1926

Book of Landscape Gardening: Treatise on the General Principles Governing Outdoor Art with Sundry Suggestions for Their Application in the Commoner Problems of Gardening. 3rd ed. New York: Orange Judd, 1926.

Frank A. Waugh and Prentiss French. "Sculptor and Landscape Architect: Daniel Chester French." *LA* 16, no. 2 (January 1926): 91–99.

"Outdoor New England." *Review of Reviews* 73 (June 1926): 611–20.

"The Present Status of Recreation Uses District 7 National Forests: Report of a Survey." Manuscript, August 1926. U.S. Forest Service.

"Stonehenge on Salisbury Plain: A National Monument in England That Sets a High Standard for America." *American Forests and Forestry Life* 32 (August 1926): 465.

"Popular Aster." *CLA* 50 (September 1926): 59–60.

"Instruction in Landscape Gardening in American Colleges." In "School News." *LA* 17, no. 1 (October 1926): 60–63.

"College Fraternity." *Review of Reviews* 74 (December 1926): 641–46.

1927

Formal Design in Landscape Architecture: A Statement of Principles with Special Reference to Their Present Use in America. New York: Orange Judd, 1927.

"A Warning." In "School News." *LA* 17, no. 3 (April 1927): 242.

"Crossing the Blue Ridge." *American Forests and Forestry Life* 33, no. 401 (May 1927): 272.

"Teaching the Beauty of Landscape." *Journal of the National Education Association* 16, no. 392 (May 1927): 137–38.

"Bull Session." *School and Society* 25, no. 647 (21 May 1927): 609–10.

1928

Hardy Shrubs: A Simple Handbook of Practical Information. New York and London: Orange Judd, 1928.

"Landscape Architecture in North America, United States and Canada: Historical and Critical Survey." In *History of Garden Art*, edited by Marie Gothein, translated by Laura Archer-Hind. 3rd ed. New York: Dutton, 1928.

"New Lilacs You'll Like." *Ladies' Home Journal* 45 (March 1928): 29.

"Trees in the Garden Picture." *CLA* 53 (March 1928): 41–43.

"Catch 'Em Young!" *GM&HB* 47 (May 1928): 275.

"Notes on Outdoor Theaters." *LA* 18, no. 4 (July 1928): 261–65.

"Blackstone Valley." *Survey Midmonthly* 60 (1 August 1928): 475.

1929

"Picketed Gardens from Cape Cod." *House & Garden* 56 (July 1929): 87.

"Instruction in Landscape Gardening in American Colleges: A Review and Criticism." *Proceedings of the International Congress of Plant Sciences*, Section of Horticulture. Ithaca, N.Y., 17 August 1929.

1930

Everybody's Garden: The How, the Why and Especially the Wherefore of the Home Garden, with Emphasis upon the Interests of the Average American. New York: Orange Judd, 1930.

"Florida of the Future—In Terms of Gardens and of Landscape Architecture." *American Landscape Architect* 2, no. 3 (February 1930): 7.

"Wilderness to Keep." *Review of Reviews* 81 (February 1930): 146, 151–52.

"Trees, Flowers and Shrubs Are Home." *Springfield Sunday Union*, 18 May 1930.

"Large Scale Planning: The Mount Hood National Forest." *American Landscape Architect* 2, no. 6 (June 1930): 20–23.

Frederick Law Olmsted, Frank A. Waugh, and John C. Merriam. "Public Values of the Mount Hood Area." In Senate Doc. 164, June 11, 1930, 71st Congress, 2nd Session.

"The Garden Celebrates Independence." *Better Homes and Gardens* 8 (July 1930): 11.

"Grounds of the Massachusetts Agricultural College." *American Landscape Architect* 3, no. 2 (August 1930): 27–30.

"Pentstemon Loco." *American Forests and Forestry Life* 36, no. 9 (September 1930): 570–71.

F. A. Waugh and C. W. Thompson. *Hardy Woody Plants. MAESB* no. 267 (October 1930).

"Why I Am Not a Pictorial Photographer." *Photo-Era* 65 (November 1930): 266–68.

1931

"Ecology of the Roadside." *LA* 21, no. 2 (January 1931): 81–92.

Experiments with Hedges. MAESB no. 272 (March 1931).

"Natural Plant Groups." *LA* 21, no. 3 (April 1931): 169–79.

"Children Need Not Be Chloroformed." *School and Society* 33 (16 May 1931): 665–67.

"Country Roads, Modern Style." *Survey Midmonthly* 66 (1 July 1931): 350–52.

"Stock of Fine Drives Enriched by New Belchertown Cut Off." *Springfield Sunday Union* (2 October 1931).

"A Juniper Landscape." *American Landscape Architect* 5, no. 5 (November 1931): 16–20.

1932

"The Physiography of Lakes and Ponds." *LA* 22, no. 2 (January 1932): 89–99.

"Pine Woods." *American Landscape Architect* 6, no. 16 (February 1932): 16–20.

"Running Water." *LA* 22, no. 4 (July 1932): 270–80.

1933

"Buildings in the National Forests." *LA* 23, no. 4 (July 1933): 263–64.

"Uncle Sam's Big Farm Race Run Off Forty Years Ago." *Springfield Sunday Union and Republican*, 10 September 1933.

"The Great 5 and 10." *Springfield Sunday Union and Republican*, 1 October 1933.

1934

Pruning and Care of Shrubbery. MAC Extension Service Leaflet no. 7, rev. ed.

"The Forest Margin." *Journal of Forestry* 32, no. 1 (January 1934): 11–14.

"Plant a Grape Vine Anywhere!" *American Home* 12 (July 1934): 98.

1935

"Some Hope for Art." *LA* 25, no. 2 (January 1935): 72–74.

Frank A. Waugh and Sidney Biehler Waugh. "American Glass to London." *Arts and Decorations* 42 (April 1935): 14.

"Landscape Conservation: Planning for the Restoration, Conservation, and Utilization of Wilds Lands for Park and Forest Recreation." Manuscript, August 1935. U.S. Department of the Interior, National Park Service.

1936

"Reconciliation of Land Use: What This Country Now Needs, Says a Noted Authority, Is a Clearer Recognition of the Principle of Reconciliation and of Its Primacy in Administrative Practices." *Journal of Land and Public Utility Economics* 12 (February 1936): 87–89.

"Landscape Conservation: Planning the Recreational Use of Our Wild Lands," chap. 1, "Objectives." *P&R* 19, no. 6 (February 1936): 177–80; chap. 2, "Site Planning." *P&R* 19, no. 7 (March 1936): 229–33; chap. 3, "Camps and Camping." *P&R* 19, no. 8 (April 1936): 272–76; chap. 4, "Sanitation." *P&R* 19, no. 9 (May 1936): 328–32; chap. 5, "The Forest Stand." *P&R* 19, no. 10 (June 1936): 379–81.

The Bulbous Iris and Its Outdoor Culture in Massachusetts. MAESB no. 330 (April 1936).

Frank A. Waugh and Arnold M. Davis. *Highway Planting.* MAC Extension Service Leaflet no. 163 (April 1936).

"Roadside Ecology – California Notes." *LA* 26, no. 3 (April 1936): 119–27.

"Those Upper Altitudes." *American Photography* 30 (May 1936): 296–98.

"Some Ecological Problems." *P&R* 19, no. 11 (July 1936): 434–36.

"Camera as an Art Accessory." *American Photography* 30 (October 1936): 648–54.

1937

Landscape Conservation: Planning for the Restoration, Conservation, and Utilization of Wilds Lands for Park and Forest Recreation. Washington, D.C.: Civilian Conservation Corps, P. T. Series no. 6.

"Hedges for All Purposes." *Better Homes and Gardens* 15 (April 1937): 20–21.

"Physical Aspects of Country Planning." *Journal of Land and Public Utility Economics* 13 (August 1937): 232.

"Campus Organization of the Fine Arts." *Bulletin of the Association of American Colleges* 23 (November 1937): 342.

1938

"Studies from the Nude." *Country Life and the Sportsman* 75 (December 1938): 60–62.

1939

"Pollard Willows." *Gardeners' Chronicles of America* 43, no. 3 (March 1939): 69.

"A Fading Remnant: Etchings of Old Sawmills." *Survey Graphic* 28 (July 1939): 434–35.

1940

"How Fare the Trees?" *House Beautiful* 82 (March 1940): 64, 112–14.

1941

Review of *Japanese Garden Construction* by Samuel Newsom. *LA* 31, no. 2 (January 1941): 89–90.

"Inspiration from the Landscape: Composition." *Proceedings of the Eighth Annual Outdoor Recreation Conference, Massachusetts State College*, Amherst, Mass., 13–16 March 1941.

1942

[John Smedley, pseud.]. *Home Pork Production; A Popular Treatise Containing Concise and Dependable Information on the Breeding, Feeding, Care and Management of Pigs to Secure the Largest Measure of Satisfaction, Pleasure and Piglets.* New York: Orange Judd, 1942.

BOOK OF
LANDSCAPE GARDENING

SUMMER IN THE GARDEN

BOOK OF LANDSCAPE GARDENING

TREATISE ON THE GENERAL PRINCIPLES GOVERNING OUTDOOR ART; WITH SUNDRY SUGGESTIONS FOR THEIR APPLICATION IN THE COMMONER PROBLEMS OF GARDENING

By FRANK A. WAUGH

Professor of Landscape Gardening, Massachusetts Agricultural College

ILLUSTRATED

NEW YORK
ORANGE JUDD PUBLISHING COMPANY
1926

Set up and Electrotyped.
Published November, 1926

Printed in the United States of America

TO

ALBERT DICKENS

PROFESSOR OF HORTICULTURE

KANSAS STATE AGRICULTURAL COLLEGE

He also loves the plains

PREFACE TO THE THIRD EDITION

When this book was first published, twenty-seven years ago, it was the work of an inexperienced boy. The fact that it found a market at that time was not surprising considering the meagerness of the literature then current in the field of landscape gardening. The more remarkable observation is that it should continue to find readers now after more than a quarter of a century has wholly changed the aspect of landscape art in this country and after hundreds of very excellent books have been added to our store.

Yet since there seem to be a good many persons who still find this elementary treatise useful it seems only fair to present a new edition with such revisions as experience may suggest. The real problem lies in making timely additions without destroying the freshness of a youthful book.

Of course the fundamental principles on which landscape architecture rests do not change, and perhaps the continued popularity of this book rests upon a certain success in the statement of those unchanging principles. The understanding of such principles seems to be about the best result which any student can get from a book. Practical experience is also indispensable, but experience must be sought outside the library.

The original edition of this work was offered timidly

enough and in a full realization of its inadequacy. As these twenty-seven years have passed and our knowledge of landscape architecture has greatly enlarged, the inadequacy of these statements has been more and more apparent to this author. Even with all possible revision it will still be impossible to cover fully the wide field of landscape gardening. Certainly the reader and the author will understand each other best if we regard the present book as a simple introduction to the simplest principles which rule in the realm of our art, and which indeed rule in a large part of our lives.

FRANK A. WAUGH.

Massachusetts Agricultural College
October 1, 1926

TABLE OF CONTENTS

PART III—GENERAL PROBLEMS

PART IV—THE GARDENER'S MATERIALS

PART V—BIBLIOGRAPHY

PART I

Introductory

CHAPTER I

THE ART AND THE ARTIST

"If now we ask when and where we need the Fine Art of Gardening, must not the answer be, whenever and wherever we touch the surface of the ground and the plants it bears with the wish to produce an organized result that shall please the eye? The name we usually apply to it must not mislead us into thinking that this art is needed only for the creation of broad 'landscape' effects. It is needed wherever we do more than grow plants for the money we may save or gain by them. It does not matter whether we have in mind a great park or a small city square, a large estate or a modest dooryard, we must go about our work in an artistic spirit if we want a good result. Two trees and six shrubs, a scrap of lawn and a dozen flowering plants, may form either a beautiful little picture or a huddled disarray of forms and colors."

Mrs. Schuyler Van Rensselaer.

Landscape gardening is eminently a fine art. The enumeration of painting, sculpture and architecture as the fine arts is seriously deficient, and yet it has a wide currency. That is a fine art which attempts to create organized beauty—to unite several dissimilar parts in one harmonious whole. In this respect landscape art stands on a level with the other fine arts. In some other respects it even surpasses them.

This art is also known as landscape architecture. Indeed landscape architecture is the term habitually used by professional workers in America, though one sometimes hears of "landscape engineering" and "landscape design." All these designations suffer from being too ponderous, and none of them is free from other objections. There has been some controversy as to which one should be certified and used, but the argument has been highly unprofitable. The ordinary student will find it best to regard all these names as synonymous.

A FORECOURT FOUNTAIN

In former times the simple word "gardening" was in general use in England to designate this art, especially that style of gardening practice known as the natural, or English, method. This would still be the most convenient word if we could dissociate it from the growing of cabbages and parsnips; but that seems impossible with us now.

The chief objections to the longer titles are that they

are too long and have too large a sound. By their very look and sonorousness they seem to suggest princely and magnificent undertakings of parks, villas and hunting grounds, and to overshoot entirely those small domestic concerns around which the most of our life and interest center. This is the difficulty we would overcome if we could get back our older and plainer word, "gardening." But landscape gardening does, nevertheless, bring itself to the consideration of these lowlier problems; and it is for the sake of such smaller cares that we need most to study its principles. All persons ought to endeavor to understand the methods and aims of landscape art, as they endeavor to master the alphabet of literature. Good taste in gardening will yield its possessor as much pleasure as good taste in architecture, poetry or music. And just as one may cultivate good taste in literature without designing to become a professional writer, so one may properly educate his taste for landscape gardening with no expectation of becoming a landscape gardener.

Gardening art offers this advantage to its lovers: that they can everywhere enjoy it, and that with comparatively small expense they can patronize it on their own account. The poor washerwoman who has hardly time to look at the statue of George Washington in the city park, and scarce money enough to buy a chromo, is quite able to grow geraniums in her windows and to have a pretty bed of marigolds and phloxes in the yard. The opportunities to cultivate a taste for this

THE AUTHOR'S GARDEN

sort of landscape art lie all about us, while to only a few comes the freedom of art galleries and exhibitions.

"Landscape gardener," "landscape architect," "landscape artist," "gardener," have their obvious relation to the terms already considered. Whatever he may be called, the practitioner of the art is an artist. He may be a good artist, or a poor one. He would face the same possibility if he were a painter.

The necessity for insisting upon this point is greater because the obsession of our age is science—something quite different from art. Thousands of good and urgent men have been sleeplessly trying to reduce every human activity and emotion to science. Not a few have striven to place gardening upon a scientific basis. Now this may do very well for the commercial production of onions, or even of hothouse roses; but the making of beautiful landscapes is not science, but art, and if we are to understand it at all we must keep these too ideas separate.

We have already tried to distinguish between the landscape artist and the layman who has a trained and sympathetic understanding of the artist's work. The layman possessed of good artistic taste and a proper horticultural knowledge can doubtless produce many beautiful and satisfactory things in his own yard; and such lay artists are sorely needed. But for real creative work of any magnitude the born and trained artist is required. Genius like that of Raphael, or Turner, is more a matter of natural endowment than of education. Genius like that of Frederick Law Olmsted is of the same order. In the following pages the prime attempt is for the cultivation of the taste of the layman. There are many things which he ought to understand, and to that end a systematic classification of principles and a somewhat didactic treatment of details may be excused.

The order and relative importance of the several principles may be understood most easily by a study of the accompanying analytical outline. It is conceived that unity, variety, motive, character, propriety and finish are the fundamental characteristics of any landscape,—that these qualities are ultimate and coördinate, though by no means equally important. Each work of landscape art is to be tested separately for each of these qualities. The following pages explain in order how these tests are to be variously satisfied.

PART II

General Principles

CHAPTER II

UNITY

Every yard should be a picture. That is, the area should be set off from every other area, and it should have such a character that the observer catches its entire effect and purpose without stopping to analyze its parts. The yard should be one thing, one area, with every feature contributing its part to one strong and homogeneous effect. *L. H. Bailey.*

Pictorial composition may be defined as the proportionate arranging and unifying of the different features and objects of a picture. . . . There must be an exercise of judgment on the part of the artist as to fitness and position, as to harmony of relation, proportion, color, light; and there must be a skilful uniting of all the parts into one perfect whole.

John C. Van Dyke.

Unity and coherence are not quite synonymous, yet the ideas are very closely related, and in any extensive composition are practically inseparable. Thus a number of objects of exactly the same sort placed together would undoubtedly secure unity without any effort for coherence; but several dissimilar objects may also be assembled in satisfying unity if, by some obvious relation or natural connection, they readily cohere.

Unity in any landscape composition means that some one idea shall prevail throughout, and that all details shall be subordinate to it. Some particular style of expression must be determined upon and consistently adhered to; and the chosen style must not be varied except within wide limits of space. Every item of the composition, then, must contribute to the perfection of the predominant style, or must be vigorously expunged, no matter what its individual excellence.

Unity is not to be realized unless the entire construction is under control of one mind, and this one directing mind must not only have a perfectly clear and definite conception of what the finished product is to be, but must also be attached to that ideal with such zeal that no item, however desirable by itself, shall be admitted if not in strictest harmony with the pervading spirit of the work.

Practically this means that a definite plan should be made on paper. The unrecorded ideal, even of the artist whose conceptions are clearest, is sure to change in time; and since it must always require a considerable season to compass any landscape plans, the first keynote is likely to have been lost before the end is reached, and the later additions are apt to be out of harmony with the earlier work. The plan should be drawn with good inks on durable paper; and it should be supplemented by written specifications made equally durable. In both plans and specifications too great care cannot be taken, nor too deep a study made of the whole and of each of its parts; for, as has already been pointed out, it is fatal to leave latitude for change of mind or to invite alterations. These plans and specifications, too, cannot descend too deeply into the details of the composition; for an unsympathetic treatment of the smallest items may mar the grandest conception.

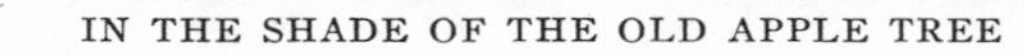

IN THE SHADE OF THE OLD APPLE TREE

Mistake is common at this point. Many people, even landscape gardeners, seem to think that if the general outlines of the plan are determined by a master artist, the construction and all minor matters may be left to the plantsman, the florist, or the man-of-all-work. On the contrary plans and specifications are not too explicit if they locate every lilac bush and spiræa and clump of columbine, and if they demand that the lilac shall be a *Frau Dammann,* the spiræa a *prunifolia,* and the columbine of the variety *Skinneri.*

It is no controversion of this statement to say, what is the undeniable fact, that the best considered plans will not always work out exactly upon the ground. It is indeed true that there are always arising, in the construction, exigencies which require this addition, that omission, or an entire change. It becomes, then, all the more important that, in all things where it is at all possible, a predetermined scheme shall be followed. The ideas of the author, conscientiously worked out in some parts, give a definite suggestion for the concordant treatment of other parts to which his foresight could not have extended. Nor is it a sufficient excuse for changing any detail of a plan that some other item seems at the time to be better than the one originally proposed, even though it be to introduce some new and beautiful plant not known to the artist. Only a few of these changes are required to alter radically the original idea, and possibly to destroy forever the unity of its expression.

Even in the smallest compositions, such as the planting of a town lot or the ornamentation of a cemetery block, a definite and explicit plan should be decided upon at the outset; it should be reduced in full to paper, and should ever after be conscientiously followed.

There are two great styles of landscape gardening,—the natural and the architectural. The former is sometimes called the English style, from the circumstance that it received its first great development at the hands of the English gardeners; and the latter is often known as the Italian style, from having been brought to a high degree of perfection by Italian artists. It is quite possible to conceive of other legitimate styles, and room is accordingly made for a method of treatment not seldom employed, called here the picturesque style. This is neither "natural," in the sense of belonging to the English school, nor in the least architectural. It is more closely akin to the Japanese style than any other; but we know so little of the Japanese style that it seems unsafe to discuss it here. This "picturesque style" is not commonly spoken of as a distinct method; yet it seems better to treat it here as such, and to point out that there may be other distinctive styles adopted in special cases, though none has yet become sufficiently prominent to be named and classified.

These several styles are, to a great degree, mutually exclusive. It is not simply that a landscape gardener is likely to be a partisan of one of the great schools,—though that is true,—but the different styles, especially

A SIMPLE HOME GARDEN IN THE FORMAL STYLE

the natural and the architectural, are utterly diverse in their objects and their methods, so that when brought together they produce nothing but discord. Within wide space limits two styles may be used, but it requires a skillful hand to effect a coherence along the line of junction. Those who remember the Wooded Island and the Court of Honor in the World's Fair grounds at Chicago, have in mind an excellent illustration of this. Even here the English was not mixed with the Italian style; but the two were separated as widely as the room permitted. One has only to imagine the architectural and sculpturesque features of the Court transferred to the midst of the Island to feel at once what a raging discord would have resulted. In the broadest terms, then, it is correct to prescribe that some one style must be chosen and consistently followed throughout the development of any landscape plan. This is the first step toward securing unity.

Unity being so important—so absolutely indispensable—we ought to consider carefully the means whereby it is gained and guarded. A careful analysis of the problem will help substantially toward this end.

First, and simplest, perhaps also most important, is unity of motive or subject matter. The meaning of motive in landscape architecture is more fully explained in Chapter IV, but it is clear enough on first statement that one subject or motive should be chosen for each composition, and that other subjects should not be mixed with it. If the gardener dedicates a small plot to the growing of roses then for its best effect as a rose garden he should exclude pansies, sunflowers, poppies, asters, lilacs, and all other favorites from this particular area. These other flowers will only be confusing, and no matter how beautiful in themselves, will detract from the unity and from the best effect of the rose garden.

The analogy between gardening and rhetoric is a close one, and it may help to remember that in all language composition unity of subject matter is especially enjoined. If one would write a lecture about the progress of forestry, for example, he must rigorously confine himself to that topic; and no matter how keen he may be to say something on prohibition or child welfare or woman's dress, he must reserve all his ideas on those subjects for another occasion. This is precisely the situation in landscape gardening, only it is not so widely understood, and so we find many persons trying to put everything into one and the same garden plot. Only confusion can result.

Next we may notice that unity of purpose saves many a composition. If we build a school grounds, for example, and every walk, tree, shrub, pump, fence, all contribute clearly and efficiently to school uses, then all these items are thereby unified. On the contrary if there are introduced some things, like a corn-crib, a tomb-stone, or a bow-knot flower-bed, not obviously necessary to the purposes of the school, unity is immediately disturbed.

As already mentioned, unity demands clearly that a single style be followed in every work of landscape gardening. The great traditional styles have their own distinguishing characteristics, and one style can not be mixed with another without disastrous results. Even quite minor styles should be kept pure.

Character is also discussed on page 52, where it is explained that in landscape gardening, character refers to the personal qualities contributed to the work by the landscape gardener. Now it is well known that one man sometimes lays out a park or an estate and that afterwards he is superseded by another park superintendent or another landscape architect. The second man has different ideas and proceeds to alter the plan to suit himself. Perhaps after he has gone his way a third man takes charge and superimposes his plan upon the two already jumbled together upon the grounds. Many examples of this sort are to be found in America and even in Europe, but it is always plain that these compromises of different men's ideas all run to the detriment of the picture. Unity of ideas, that is of character, would be much better.

Design is the very essence of landscape architecture. The landscape architect is ever trying to bring his materials together in some sort of order or design. This means literally that he is trying to build unity out of diversity, probably retaining his diversity at the same time. So he divides his land into areas of sundry sizes and shapes, he builds enclosures, plants borders, lays out walls, and builds up patterns of all kinds. But if his design is successful the success lies precisely in building a structure of such strength and

A GREEK VASE AS A GARDEN FEATURE

obvious unity that all parts of his composition are firmly held together.

Color unity is much discussed in gardening circles. One lady wants a blue garden; another thinks pink would better match her new dress from Paris. The point is that color schemes and color harmonies all tend toward unity. It is better to have all blue flowers in a garden than to have a mess of everything; and it is much better to have soft yellow day-lilies harmonizing with pale blue larkspurs than to have pink roses making faces at the magenta blossoms of Anthony Waterer spirea.

Unity of form is quite as important in landscape architecture as color unity—perhaps more so. Elm trees and spruce trees, for example, have nothing in common with respect to form, and they do not harmonize when planted together. These similarities and unlikenesses should be thoughtfully observed and care taken to secure unity of forms in planting.

In architectural forms unity is even more obviously necessary. A group of farm buildings may all look alike and produce together a pleasing effect; or they may all be of different design, giving only a disheartening disharmony. On a college campus, for another example, it is plain that the effect is much better if all buildings have unity of form and architectural style. Twenty different buildings of twenty different kinds make an ugly campus, no matter if each particular building is a gem of its kind.

Finally it may be noted that the last term in unity

is monotony. Yet whereas monotony usually has a bad reputation, in actual practice it is often salutary and pleasing. A small garden full of nothing but Festiva Maxina peony is a grand sight. And what can be more beautiful than a piece of woods of pure white pines? A hedge is a thousand times handsomer if made all of arbor vitae than though arbor vitae were mixed with privet, hemlock, buckthorn, spruce, caragana, acanthopanax and twenty other species, all of them good hedge plants when used alone.

So the landscape architect sometimes welcomes monotony. In certain situations it is a sure refuge—a very proper expedient.

But whether motive unity, or style unity, or color harmony, or final and complete monotony, unity is our prime requirement. Without unity there can be no landscape gardening.

CHAPTER III

VARIETY

Nature puts so much variety into her reality that she is more beautiful than we can imagine by sheer force of quantity! Ten days for an artist in a mountain valley will give him ten views from the same point which will be entirely different each day.

F. Schuyler Mathews.

Gettiamo un rapido sguardo sul vasto imperio delle arti, osserviamo per poco le produzioni di ciascuna, e resteremo convitti che, nulla e bello alla ragione se non le si presenta con parti varie, e queste riunite in un principo comune.

F. Cartolano.

Many of the ancient treatises on art, and some of the moderns, have summed up everything in unity with variety. These two principles plainly stand in a position of commanding importance to the whole field of art. They also bear a special relation to one another.

Unity is commonly conceded to be the most indispensable, yet if unity means uniformity, sameness, the eye soon tires of it. But unity does not demand sameness. There may be unity with variety. The two are not really opposed to each other, though either one would be easier to accomplish could the other be disregarded. Perfect unity with satisfying variety need not be even a compromise; but both tests must always be applied by the gardener. It is helpful to the landscape composer to remember that variety is possible in motive, surface, form, materials, color, texture, season, composition and position. We shall now briefly consider the possibilities of these modifications.

With respect to motive, theme or subject matter (see page 44 for further explanation) it is clear that an endless catalog of subjects awaits the landscape architect's handiwork. He may find his theme in different kinds of land, as dune-land, prairie, forest, lakeshore, mountains, brooks, etc. Or he may find it in the multitudious species of noble trees ready to his hand; for example, oaks, the white pine, the royal palm, the eucalyptus, the deodar, the apple tree or even the transitory Lombardy poplar. One garden may have the peony for its motive, another may flame with poppies, another may ring all the delightful changes upon the iris theme; while rose gardens have enjoyed to themselves an almost immemorial reputation. Some knowledge of materials is necessary in order to choose motives wisely, and some imagination to present them with artistic conviction; but the opportunity for variety is so great that no gardener ought to be excused for anything trite or commonplace.

In seeking to vary the surface on which our gardening is to be done, our attention falls first upon the three simplest forms of ground, viz., the plane, the concave and the convex surfaces. And we note also that the concave and convex surfaces give in themselves a much greater variety of view than is afforded by a plane. This is so potent a principle that in making up the surface of the grounds for park or residence purposes great care is usually taken to avoid a perfect plane, and still to give a uniform swell or depression. Breaking the plane with a succession of little hillocks would be fatal indeed. Of these three classes of surface the concave is usually to be preferred

PLEASING VARIETY IN STREET PLANTING

for small areas, for it gives much the best effect of extent. From any point within a concavity the whole surface is visible. This is not true of a convexity; and a perfectly flat surface will, unless given some bold and striking treatment, always have a suggestion of inconsequentiality about it.

A caution needs to be inserted here to secure the best use of these several varieties of surface. As long ago as 1770 Thomas Wheatley said: "In made ground the connection is, perhaps, the principal consideration. A swell which wants it is but a heap; a hollow but a hole; and both appear artificial. . . . Such shapes should be contiguous as most readily unite; and the actual division between them should be anxiously concealed. If a swell descends upon a level; if a hollow sinks from it, the level is an abrupt termination, and a little rim marks it distinctly. To cover that rim a short sweep at the foot of the swell, a small rotundity at the entrance of the hollow, must be interposed." All these cautions are fully worth attention, for the slightest differences in the surface of the ground are obvious and important to the sensitive beholder.

Broken ground offers an evident and spicy variety. The value of broken ground for developments of the picturesque is to be especially considered.

Sloping grounds have a value all their own, and for their most effective utilization, require a special treatment. For the present we will content ourselves by saying that two opportunities are afforded the gardener by sloping grounds which are elsewhere unusual. The first is in the diversity of surface presented. The second is in the advantageous situation for the display of many plants which, in any other position, would not appear to advantage. In respect to the first, it should be explained that even comparatively gentle slopes may be emphasized by proper treatment until they appear to be steep declivities. The first expedient to this end lies in the treatment of the ground itself. It is simply to contrive small irregularities of the surface by placing here and there a little swell which rises abruptly and then falls away very gently down the hill. This part of the declivity will of course be steeper than the general slope; and a few of these contrasts will give the appearance desired. Such variety is often to be sought on a nearly flat and featureless place. A slope also furnishes a specially suitable location for the disposition of rocks, both because they are needed to hold the hillside against washing by rains, and because they appear to much better advantage than on level ground. If the rocks used on a hillside are not in their natural stratifications, and plainly so, they should always be covered, or nearly so, with grass and shrubs and trailing vines. Many trailing vines give great satisfaction if allowed to run at liberty down the side of a bank.*

Water in any form furnishes an ever pleasing addition to a garden, whether as a bubbling fountain, a sparkling brook, or a cool and quiet expanse of mirror-like surface. In brooks and ponds it furnishes one of the most delightful resources of the landscape gardener. Besides the wonderful variety of pleasing effects of which it is in itself capable, it provides the only opportunity for growing many species and varie-

*Trailing plants may often be used to great advantage. In many such situations the hardy perennials are especially desirable. There is to be considered also the great possibilities of rock gardening—an entire field by itself, and a fascinating one.

ties of our most beautiful plants. The possibilities which are open to the landscape gardener in the treatment of water surfaces are so magnificent and manifold that neither description nor enumeration is practicable here. We can only declare with all emphasis that when water surfaces are brought into a landscape composition an immeasurable field of pleasing variety is opened for cultivation by the resourceful gardener.

A curved line changes direction at every point. This is the old definition, which, in itself, is a plain statement that an infinite variety of direction is contained in a curved line. A straight line has only one direction.

The partial concealment of principal points of interest is a common and profitable expedient in most cases,—less so perhaps in the architectural style than in others. In the natural style it is always admissible to group the trees so as to hide, partially or totally, the buildings from certain points of view, and to give a really complete view from only a few specially favorable points. If a tree group is so placed as to afford a partial view of the buildings from one standpoint, a totally different view is seen from a second standpoint. In this way the buildings are seen in a great variety of forms. If a drive or walk leads up to some object of special interest, it may always be considered a good plan, where possible, to give successive glimpses of the object along the way, reserving a full view for a final triumph at a point from which the whole may be best admired.

Deep vistas in any landscape planting are desirable for many reasons. They give perspective to the picture. Our gardening is usually on too small a scale to satisfy fully the hungry eye. One's look will wander away and beyond the fence which limits the little garden, and seek to lose itself at the farthest reach of the eyesight's power. Thus it but satisfies a natural desire if the openings in the garden plantings are so placed as to permit the eye full enjoyment of any good extraneous view. And even within the grounds a long perspective supplies a variety of views, since in it some objects are seen at a distance, some in middle-ground and some in the foreground.

The sky line should never be monotonous. In picturesque effects the sky line may be much broken. The charm of the purely natural style, on the contrary, especially in certain situations, lies in its utter quietness and peacefulness. A horizon full of Lombardy poplar exclamation points is not in key with such ideas. But the sky line may be diversified more gently. It may be carried high on one side by a mass of heavy woods; it may sink low on another side, to the surface of a lake; and in one or two places it may perhaps be accentuated with the spire-like poplars. This is a matter in which good taste must be exercised; for while very few observers will analyze a scene and itemize the excellencies and defects of the sky line, the sympathetic mind will be keenly, though perhaps unconsciously, alive to both.

Very few people have any conception of the multitudinous species and varieties of trees, shrubs, climbers, flowering and foliage plants at the command of the horticultural architect. With twenty sorts of maples, and as many oaks; with poplars in all shapes and sizes; with dozens of varieties of lilacs, scores of spiræas and hundreds of roses; with evergreens and deciduous trees; fastigiate and weeping trees; dark-colored and yellow trees; broad-leaved and cut-leaved trees; big trees and little trees; with other trees, shrubs, climbers and hardy plants literally "too numerous to mention," the gardener need never want for variety of material. To know these resources and to understand the possibilities of each species and variety is to master the landscape gardener's useful alphabet.

"From the artistic point of view, trees have three characteristics which may be separately studied,—form, texture and color."* We have already noticed the general variety in forms available to the landscape gardener; but it is worth while, in the present connection, to emphasize the attractive variety of forms which meet the admiration of the tree lover. The form of a tree is its first and most evident characteristic. Its outline is always beautiful, either in its symmetry or its irregularity, as the case may be; and the man who does not notice the difference between the form of a Sugar maple and a Mossy Cup oak is one to whom the Sistine Madonna might as well have been a chromo.

---

*Mrs. Schuyler Van Rensselaer, "Art Out of Doors."

There are considerable contrasts of color among trees. One may cite as examples the Red oak, the Silver poplar and the Golden willow. But the most pleasing and numerous varieties of color in trees and shrubs are separated from each other as barely distinguishable tints. The proper combination of these tints is delicate work for a sympathetic and artistic mind; but there is, nevertheless, a wide difference between good combinations and bad ones.

The difference between a strip of mosquito netting and a piece of sail cloth is chiefly one of texture. We speak of texture oftenest in connection with woven fabrics, and in that connection we best understand what it means. But it is not a difficult matter to transfer this notion of texture to the apparent solidity, or lack of solidity, in the mass of green which the foliage of any tree presents. A plane tree is not greatly different in form from a Kentucky coffee tree, and yet what a vast difference in the effect they have on the observer! Compare a catalpa with a honey locust; a tulip tree with a willow. What a difference in the whole aspect of the trees contrasted! These examples may, perhaps, suggest the meaning of Mrs. Van Rensselaer's definition: "By texture of a tree I mean the character of its masses of foliage as determined by the manner of growth of the lighter spray, and the number, shape, disposition and tissue of its leaves." In no other quality of a tree is variety more effective than in the texture.

The horticultural calendar has certain well-marked

A GARDEN PICTURE IN THE DESERT

divisions to which the exhibitor of growing plants may well have thoughtful regard. The first essay that was ever written in the English language on the subject of ornamental gardening opened with an extreme prescription for this arrangement. "I do hold it," says Bacon,* "in the royal ordering of gardens, there ought to be gardens for all the months of the year, in which, severally, things of beauty may be then in season." The essayist proceeds immediately to give a catalogue of the plants seasonable to each month of the year, "for the climate of London." We may doubt whether ten or twelve classes of plants can practicably be made on this basis; but we distinguish in our own feelings with great differences between spring greens, June roses, midsummer's wealth of foliage, autumn colors and winter scenes. Any particular plant is not likely to figure in its perfection through more than one or two of these seasons; and this opens to the landscape gardener a serious problem. The question is, shall we attempt to intermingle the perfections of all the year so as to have somewhat of attractiveness in each several group at all times? Or shall we rather follow the prescription of Lord Bacon, and group together those plants suitable to each successive season? Doubtless each method is at times expedient. If one's garden is so small as to hold only a single group of plants he will scarcely care to buy a single month of superlative perfection at the expense of eleven months of dullness and

*Lord Francis Bacon, Essays, "Of Gardening."

desolation. But where the gardening is on a more extensive scale the artist may distribute his beauties into any sort of an annual cyclorama which he chooses. He will gain, at all events, a most acceptable variety by having regard to the special seasons mentioned.

It is not within the range of our present inquiry to enumerate those special plants which are ready to the gardener's hand for these diverse effects. This has already been done in many useful books, and some suggestions are made in Chapters XIX-XXIV of the present volume. The competent gardener should be able, out of his own knowledge, to select the most pleasing materials for his pictures.

The light gray-greens are perhaps characteristic of the early spring. As trees and shrubs put forth their first unfolding buds the general effect is much different from that given by the same plants after the full dress of foliage is put on. Usually the color is several shades lighter—grayer—and this appearance is further heightened by the grayer twigs not yet covered out of sight but showing more and more dimly through the thickening screen of green leaves. Certain plants are more beautiful in this spring dress than at any subsequent season.

Some of the willows should be prominently mentioned in this category; for example, the Royal willow, *Salix regalis.* Among the smaller flowering plants there is a specially rich field of possibilities, including crocus, narcissus, jonquils, hyacinths, tulips and others. These are suitable not only to be the first occupants of the bleak flower beds after the mulch is removed in the spring, but they should be scattered with a liberal hand through the grass and in the borders, where they come on year after year amid surroundings which make them seem even more dainty and graceful and delightful harbingers of returning spring than when grown in specially prepared beds.

June is the month of roses, brides and college graduates. It is particularly a month of fêtes and carefree enjoyment of living. Weddings and commencements are the gardener's good patrons, and for them the grounds may well put on their holiday attire. June is the youthful gala time of the garden; and the bold and blushing, smiling and nodding, vain and conscious roses, which would be thought immodest amid the tranquillity of summer or the somberness of autumn, are now received with gladness as the fitting expression of our exuberant emotions. Flowers in abundance, with roses predominating; bright colors and heavy perfumes; with blacks and grays and old folks kept in the back ground—these are the colors for the June picture, the chords for the June music.

In midsummer nothing is more delightful than quiet rest under cooling shade. No flashing colors for us now. No jarring contrasts for the tired eyes. The trees now invite us with their thickest canopy of foliage; and if beneath them stretches a cool, clean greensward, and if the shadows fall all untroubled into a still pool near by, we rest amid these scenes with an overflowing gratitude for the kind hands by which they are provided. We have fled the dusty highway, the burning streets, the noise and hurry and commotion of business. Quiet and solitude are our chief desires. These feelings, common to all men at such times, indicate unequivocally the duty of the gardener.

EVEN WINTER LOOKS WELL IN THE GARDEN

With so unmistakable a demand upon him, he is no gardener at all who will not know what he ought to do.

The beautiful colors of autumn are too much looked upon as secondary qualities of the plants which affect them, and their disposition on the grounds is too much a matter of chance. The gardener ought to recognize in these autumn colors another opportunity for the aggregation of scattered beauties. Through these he may produce one more quite spectacular effect before the winter shuts us all indoors away from the enjoyment of his works.

Without speaking of the individual excellencies of the oaks, the liquidambar, the maples and the tulip trees, we may note that two distinct colors appear in great quantities, namely the reds and the yellows. Each of these is present in comparative purity in certain species, and their combination is specially adapted to provide the most extraordinary contrasts. And at no other time of the year would the eye accept such gaudy hues,—no, not even in June,— much less delight in them. But now as our overcoats are buttoned on and as we hurry along to get ourselves under shelter from the boisterous wind, we are in no mood to note details and examine delicate effects. A picture must cry out after us if it would get our attention. And so the gardener may mass together as much as he pleases of those gorgeous colors of the early frost; and we will stop a moment to admire his work again and to thank him for it ere we betake ourselves to the heated house and the absorbing book.

But even the winter does not wholly rob the gardener of his opportunity to please us. Indeed, some of the most gracious products of the ornamental grounds are those blessings which are enjoyed in midwinter. It is a mistake to suppose that the garden must be all bleakness and desolation as soon as snow falls. There is a whole host of the evergreens to refute such a supposition. The variety of them is greater than the uninitiated might at all suspect. With them may be arranged many shrubs and small trees which, though deciduous, have bark of such bright and pleasing hues that they may be shown against dark backgrounds in many cheery combinations. Such are the Golden willow, the Golden spiræa and the Red branched dogwood. A long list of others might easily be made. There are certain corners of the garden which are usually especially conspicuous from the windows of the living rooms; and it is a pity if part of this scene at least cannot be robbed of its winter bleakness. If such spots are chosen for beautiful winter effects the designer has gained another triumph.

There is some danger that the beginner in plant grouping will make all his groups alike. This is a very easy thing to do. To avoid it, it first becomes necessary that the operator shall see the sameness into which he is falling. This he can best do in his own work by directing his imagination to construct before him the various finished groups. It is certainly unlikely that the individual plants will be placed in exactly homologous positions unless the groups are set with a tape measure. But it is not difficult, if the imagination be serviceable, to compare the probable final effects of two groups, and determine with satisfactory accuracy if the two will look alike twenty years hence. Aside from the ability to see mistakes, it requires an inventive mind to devise new arrangements for groups;

but a variety of arrangements they certainly should have in any scheme not intentionally formal.

Single trees or shrubs appear to great advantage when properly placed, and if in all respects good, they add sensibly to the composite beauty of the scene. A single plant will naturally receive more and better attention when standing by itself than though it were in a group with others. For this reason it should have greater individual excellence. It should be faultless, if that can be. There are many positions about any extensive grounds in which single trees or shrubs will be acceptable units of the composition. The judgment of the designer must point these cut; but we may take note that they will usually be comparatively closer to the observer, so that the single plants will always be under critical examination. Such places are, then, to be reserved for specially choice specimens. Any rare or remarkable plant,—not monstrous and deformed,—should be given such a place of prominence. And every specimen plant should be remarkable for its individual perfections of good culture.

There are a great many general and common forms given to groups, but their classification and discussion do not belong here. It is sufficient to repeat that this is another point at which variety is both possible and proper.

There are, of course, some objects which are seen both near by and at a distance. But in the majority of instances an object,—for instance, a tree,—will be most often seen from the same distance. If it stand

THE SKY AND THE SUNSHINE ADD BEAUTY TO THE GARDEN

at the back of a wood belt, with numerous smaller trees between it and the distant roadway, it may be fairly considered in the background. On the other hand, if it stand close beside a much frequented path or just before the windows of the living room, it is usually seen in the foreground. Between these extremes there is a middle-ground of greater or less extent. The same plant gives exceedingly diverse effects as seen in these three different positions.

A background is made up most naturally of large trees. Here can be used many species of rough and irregular growth which would not look respectable at close range. Trees of which the texture is so coarse as to be inadmissible in the foreground, seem at the background to give but a gentle touch to the otherwise unbroken and monotonous surface. Trees of which the colors would jar upon a fastidious eye if seen too close, seem modest and pretty at a greater distance. Moreover, a background must be made up with due thought to the most effectual exhibition of whatever lies between it and the observers. For this reason it must not have a bristling sky line if smooth and roundheaded smaller trees are to appear in front of it. And the opposite mistake must be guarded against. One time with another, the background may best be darker than those groups which intervene between it and the usual point of view. This rule cannot always be adhered to, for it would force all dark colored species out of the fore and middle-ground; but the reverse presentation must always be looked upon as less desirable.

In the foreground, where all plants are under comparatively close scrutiny, only those should be used which will bear such examination. Flowering shrubs and herbaceous plants may be used here. In most cases plants for the foreground must be small; and though we like to have large trees next the walk so that we can enjoy their shade, and though this demand should be met, to a degree, yet a tree so placed adds nothing to the picture, and too many such trees shut off the view entirely. It is a common fault, in the plantings along drives and walks, that they do not give a satisfactory view of the landscape.

There is a great wealth of medium sized trees and large shrubs which look well in middle-ground. Of these are the buckeyes, altheas, lilacs, and the interesting kœlreuteria. The middle-ground is an advantageous place for the exhibition of all tree specimens. If the form of a tree specimen is to be admired it will be put far back in the middle-ground; if it is the beautiful foliage, it will come to the nearer middle-ground. Middle-ground plantings sometimes serve the purposes of background to foreground plantings; and this contingency is always to be kept in mind.

It not infrequently occurs that there are beautiful objects visible from the grounds under treatment and yet lying wholly outside them. It may be mountain scenery, a lake, a view of the ocean, a glimpse of a pretty village, or any other exterior object which bears an interest to the users of the grounds but which is itself wholly beyond the control of the designer. Sometimes these exterior objects are of commanding importance, as, for example, when a houselot fronts on the ocean. In such an extreme case the intelligent gardener will seek to make his entire work contribute to enhance the beauty or effectiveness of the chief object. This means, of course, that all his effects shall be subordinate to the principal interest. It would be a blameworthy act to place anything in the garden which would draw attention to itself and away from the outside view. In any case he will have careful regard to these exterior views, and will arrange his groupings so as to avail himself of whatever extraneous beauties may be at hand.

This, of course, means the leaving of open vistas along well-chosen lines. The lines which are thus to be left open, as well as all the long vistas or perspectives which are to be preserved inside the grounds, should be marked first on the paper plans, and as the plans are developed all obstructions may be kept off them. Again, when the plans are being worked out on the grounds these open lines should be carefully marked and the plantings kept at a proper distance.

CHAPTER IV

MOTIVE

What makes a garden?
Flowers, grass and trees,
Odor, grace and color:
Lovely gifts like these.
Caroline Giltinan.

Motive, theme, subject are all names given to the one principle, namely the principle that each work of art must have one idea. In high schools and colleges pupils write "themes"; and this metonymy plainly signifies that the subject matter is considered the most important feature of the exercise. Each essay must be written about one "theme," and all irrelevant matter must be strictly excluded. So the theme, subject or motive of this student essay may be dairying, the tariff in politics, George Washington or golf; but an essay without a theme would be pure foolishness.

In exactly the same way the musician uses themes. He calls them either themes or motives; sometimes he even speaks of them as subjects. In music a theme is that central recognizable figure which runs through the whole composition and the development of which is the chief concern of the composer.

In painting the use of themes or motives is as obvious as in literature. In short, we are to consider the selection and development of themes as a vital necessity in all branches of art, including landscape architecture.

But what does a theme in landscape architecture look like? Would we know one if we saw it? Let us answer this by two illustrations.

For the first let us suppose that we have a park of 40 acres on which the white pine is the predominating growth. Good landscape design would immediately suggest that we make this species the chief feature of our development. So we first of all cut out scattering weed-trees and bushes which obscure the pines or hinder their growth, and next we give ourselves to the unqualified cultivation of the chosen favorite. Now we endeavor to make the most of this motive by developing it in a variety of ways. At one point we preserve a fine picturesque single specimen of old seed pine; at another we form a group of normal mature trees; at a third point we show a broad mass of the young trees luxuriantly growing, with their soft, silky, gray-green foliage; and somewhere within this park we will of course want a dense stand of large trees, with a heavy carpet of needles beneath our feet, where we may enjoy the serene beauty of that special picture. So in various ways we exhibit the versatile beauties of the white pine motive.

For the second example of landscape motive we may assume an estate through which runs a considerable brook. Certainly we would want to make the most of so gracious a feature. To do this we would probably

AN OLD SEED PINE WITH ITS CHILDREN ABOUT IT

conduct our main walk or drive along the brook bank. The walk would not exactly parallel the brook, but would sometimes approach the stream, sometimes fall back into the woods at a little distance. At one or two specially chosen points it would cross the brook, and from these crossings probably the very best views would be seen. In one section the brook would lie quietly in deep shadows; in another it would glisten in the sun; in one place it would tumble loudly over rocks; in another it would form a deep still pool. The brook would be our motive or theme, and our landscape gardening would consist in getting out of it as many beautiful pictures as possible, in as great a variety as circumstances would allow. We would thus have a variety of views with unity of motive.

The pine-tree theme described above may be called a species motive. It is representative of a large and important class. For what we have done with the pine tree we may do with oak trees, or with maples, or with eucalyptus. Or if we make a rose garden all of roses, the way a rose garden ought to be made, then plainly we are handling a rose motive. Or if we make an iris garden, or a peony garden, or a garden of water lilies, our motive in each case is one species, genus or group of plants. Such species motives are easy to manage; they are artistically good, and they ought oftener to be adopted.

The brook may be classified as a topographic motive. Other topographic motives are often useful in landscape gardening. For example, a lake, or even a lake

INTERIOR OF THE PINE WOODS

shore, may become the highly desirable subject matter of our work. A sand dune has many beauties; and a very acceptable park might be made on sand dunes. A steep, rocky slope has its own good points and possibilities; it may be effectively planted with suitable trees, shrubs, vines and blossoming plants; it may be climbed by convenient paths; and altogether it may be treated by the landscape architect so as to be a thing of beauty and a joy forever.

It may be noted further that in the examples used for illustration there has been pointed out the regular method of using motives in landscape gardening. The pine tree is presented in a variety of aspects—at one point the single specimen tree, at another the simple group. These several sections of our composition we may call paragraphs or episodes. Just as we divide our essay into paragraphs when we write a "theme," so we develop our motive in paragraphs when we do a good job of landscape designing. In each paragraph we try to give a different treatment; and this statement holds true whether we are speaking of rhetoric or of gardening.

And further we would always need to arrange these paragraphs in some logical order. The first would be an introductory section, presenting the subject for public attention, but not expounding it. The last section would be a summary or a climax. At any rate the best paragraph—the climax—would be reserved to some point near the end. Between the introduction and the last paragraph there would be others present-

THE BROOK MOTIVE IN EARLY SPRING

ing the different features of the motive, but always, if possible, with accumulating force.

It is clear, or ought to be, that this matter of selecting good motives and developing them with the utmost effect is one which requires much knowledge, skill and experience. It is quite impossible to explain in detail all about it in a short elementary text book. But the very great importance of the motive will be evident; and it may not be too much to hope that the student, by long observation and much study, will come to understand better what is here involved, and that when he undertakes the practice of landscape gardening it may be with due humility, considering how complex and serious the whole art really is.

CHAPTER V

CHARACTER — PROPRIETY

> Although that delicacy of organization, usually called taste, is a natural gift, which can no more be acquired than hearing can be by a deaf man, yet, in most persons, this sensibility to the beautiful may be cultivated and ripened into good taste by the study and comparison of beautiful productions in nature and art.
>
> *Andrew Jackson Downing.*

Character is the most elusive quality of all those with which we deal. Almost all writers on gardening have talked more or less of character, assuming it as a quality, but never approaching a definition or an explanation. Thomas Wheatley did, in fact, long ago introduce a chapter "Of Character" into his remarkably clear analytical outline; but the chapter treated of subjects quite different from those discussed here. If I may venture on the dangerous experiment of a definition, I will say that I intend to suggest by the term character those more delicate distinctions in the general method of treatment, such as may mark one composition from another, even of the same general style. We understand clearly what is meant by character in a man or woman, and I should like to transfer this notion undisturbed to use in the descriptions of gardens. It is a common saying that the face of such and such an acquaintance is pretty but it lacks character. It is perfectly conceivable that a garden might be faultless in the unity and the harmony of its appointments, with everything beautiful and appropriate withal, and yet lack character.

In different words, we might say that character is the personal impress of the designer. Thus we would never expect a poem of pure and lofty character to flow from a wicked heart. We would not expect a painting of great power to originate in a dull, unsensitive mind. No more can we hope to see vigor and dignity displayed in a garden designed by a weak and puerile author. In this close and proper connection of the character of the garden with the character of its designer we may perhaps more clearly understand its present signification.

Misapprehension may easily arise in the use of this term, due to the fact that the same quality in literature is called style. Thus we expect the style of H. L. Mencken to be his own and to be distinctly and always different from the style of John Burroughs. Unfortunately this word "style" is already appropriated in landscape gardening to another meaning; but the personal quality which makes style in literature shows its results equally in the realm of gardening. Let us recognize it, welcome it and call it character.

Certain terms are commonly associated in criticism of gardens, such as simplicity, dignity, boldness. These I take to represent different types of character. I think this is the use commonly made by those who

THE QUIET LANDSCAPE APPROPRIATE TO THE CEMETERY

apply them to art compositions, even though those who use them thus have never stopped to generalize under any common term the qualities expressed. These terms, simplicity, dignity, and boldness, are sufficiently suggestive of certain characters. This list is not intended to be complete, for, theoretically at least, there may be an indefinite variety of character. The term complexity is added to the list only because it seems to be implied in simplicity. Perhaps elaborateness would be preferred to complexity as a term for a more careful classification.

Between the terms propriety and appropriateness it is hard to choose the better. The latter is the more explicit in its suggestions, but the former has the advantage of brevity and of good associations, which I think ought to be operative in our criticisms of taste in gardening. For as we inquire whether this or that social appointment is marked by strict propriety, so ought we to criticise the items of the gardener's work. It must be said that such criticism is sorely needed, and that many gardeners of some reputation seem never to have reflected that such a test as propriety can be applied to their work. Our American cemeteries are often striking exemplifications of this statement. In them one continually meets objects of such childish conception, such incongruous effect or such gaudy color, as to jar on nerves of any appreciative person. Much has been said and written on the subject of cemetery ornamentation, and we may assume that we are on the way to inculcate a better taste in this respect.

Although every tenet of gardening art is habitually violated in our cemeteries, the most common and disagreeable violations are doubtless instances of disregard for propriety. The matters introduced are not appropriate to the place.

But this is only a single class of improprieties, and is mentioned chiefly for illustration. Propriety is a

A SNUG GARDEN HOME IN ENGLAND

universal test. Every object and group of objects must submit to it. Thus we would often consider an aviary, or a zoological collection, or a suite of dog kennels inadmissible in a garden because they were inappropriate to the surroundings, even though they might be in themselves beautiful and interesting.

I wish to speak here again of a particular class of

improprieties to which I have already alluded, namely, the prominent display of monstrous or deformed horticultural specimens. Deformity and monstrosity have a strange fascination to uncultured minds; and there is no more unequivocal testimony to a general poverty of cultivated taste in gardening than the constantly recurring sight of such disfigurements in the gardens of people whose houses are furnished inside with scrupulous taste and propriety. It is surpassingly strange that the city resident, who has room between his house and the street for only a single specimen, will choose for that position the one plant which offers the most blemishes, as though Æsop were better to look upon than Apollo. The commonest vagary of this sort is the little weeping tree, in which the writhing agonies of one monstrous variety are grafted on the top of some straight, courageous stock for better exhibition. As one passes along a residence street in almost any town seeking something in the gardens to admire, how often must he decide that this and that plant was used because it was a freak rather than because it was beautiful or appropriate. It seems to the present scribe that propriety is the one thing to be chiefly studied by that large and needy class of Americans who have houses of their own with small grounds attached.

CHAPTER VI

FINISH

> Both richness and polish will, to a certain extent, be the result of keeping. . . . Extreme thinness of plants in beds skirting a lawn, an inferior order of plants in the neighborhood of the house or by the sides of the grass glades, and the use of commonplace or uncongenial ornaments, are inconsistent with richness.
>
> *Edward Kemp.*

No one will have read so far as this chapter without having observed the outline which the text attempts to follow. As indicated in that outline, it has been conceived that there are six distinct artistic qualities, in which any ornamental planting may be good or bad. These are unity, variety, motive, character, propriety and finish. These are all in some degree essential; but it will strike the reader at once that they are not all equally important. Those things which are here included under the unsatisfactory term "finish," are not of such paramount and continual necessity as those discussed under unity, for instance. And yet one may understand, without puzzling, that any sort of an art composition may answer all the requirements thus far set forth, and yet fail to yield a due satisfaction because it lacks a painstaking finish. Besides, one may note this defect in the concrete only too easily among pictures, books or landscapes.

In gardening, finish means several things, some of which we may designate here. In the first place, it requires good specimens. All the plants employed must be good of their kind; the minor groups must be good; and the masses must be good. The individual plants must be excellent in proportion to their conspicuousness. If a single specimen of some rare and

A WELL-APPOINTED HOME GARDEN

striking species stands in a prominent place, it cannot be permitted to wear a decrepit, unthrifty, untidy appearance. But besides this, it should have positive excellence to its credit. It should be a plant worth seeing, not merely as a botanical curiosity, but an example of nature's best work.

Good care is required to keep trees thrifty, to keep plants growing vigorously and luxuriantly. Cultivation and manure are needed. Pruning must be done. Crowded clumps must be thinned out. Sheared trees must be kept sheared, and mowed lawns must be kept mowed. The walks and drives must be kept graded and surfaced and free from weeds. Buildings must be kept painted, and fences put together and standing straight. And dozens of similar matters demand constant attention, or directly the finish of the composition is marred and its whole effectiveness diminished.

Perhaps cleanliness is only a matter of good care; but it sometimes happens that a gardener becomes so absorbed in taking good care of his shrubs and flower beds that he forgets the general cleanliness of his grounds. In public parks the lawns and walks rapidly become littered with papers and rubbish of all sorts, and this may quickly reach such a point as to interfere seriously with the satisfaction of the park users. In the farm yard, where good attempts at ornamental gardening are often made, a proper regard for cleanliness would suggest that a wheelbarrow should not be left standing in front of the house unused for a week, and that chicken coops, dog kennels, grindstones and other agricultural paraphernalia should be put behind the main dwelling house, or at least kept off the lawn. On any grounds more or less litter is bound to accumulate, and this may readily amount to enough to spoil the best studied effects of unity, variety, character and propriety.

This matter is of greater practical concern than the uninstructed person will readily imagine. In the management of city parks, for example, finish is more important, practically, than primary design. In park work this is called maintenance, and maintenance is what costs money. Consider for a moment that the ordinary city spends something like $500 an acre a year—often more—for the maintenance of its parks. Here we have a measure of what cleanliness and good order are worth to the average citizen in his own housekeeping. For good maintenance is merely good housekeeping, and good housekeeping means just what we here designate as finish.

Yet after the landscape gardener has done everything within his power, has gathered the last item of horticultural excellence, and has disposed of it with the artist's happiest effect, he is still dependent, in a very great measure, on the favor of the unmanageable elements for the results. No one will see a delicately penciled sky line or a softly harmonized background through a blinding dust storm; and a bed of finest roses is apt to look very sorry and drabbled in the midst of a cold rain. Differences in sunshine, light and atmosphere make very surprising differences in the effect of landscape views; and as far as possible, all this should be taken into account by the gardener when he makes his plan.

And besides the modifying influence which light and atmosphere exercise on landscape views, they are themselves often a very important part of the picture. Who cares to look at anything else on a day when an early, feathery snow fills the buoyant atmosphere with a delightful, softening, luminous, hush-compelling haze? And sometimes there are clouds and a sunset as beautiful as the woods or as sublime as the ocean. These do not belong to the gardener, but they may fit into his picture, and enhance the pleasure which it gives; and shall he not appropriate whatever of them he can?

A WELL-KEPT LAWN COOL WITH SHADOWS

Everyone knows that the landscape painter spends his chiefest pains to give accurate representations and stirring suggestions of light and atmosphere; but the landscape gardener has the real commodities in unmeasured, ever-shifting variety. Let him make all possible use of them, and if the elements are commonly unpropitious, as they are in some countries, he may have his proper doubts about the practicability of undertaking any gardening plans at all. Fortunately almost every country, whatever its shortcomings, has some good qualities of climate which may be studied and turned to advantage.

CHAPTER VII

THE NATURAL STYLE

> In the English landscape garden one sees and feels everywhere the spirit of nature, only softened and refined by art. In the French or Italian garden one sees and feels only the effect of art, slightly assisted by nature.
>
> *Andrew Jackson Downing.*

We ought now to consider more carefully what is implied in the leading styles of landscape gardening.

The natural style is unquestionably the favorite in England and America. This means not alone that the landscape gardeners of these countries practice it in preference to other styles, but also that the laity, composed of people who only feel and do not think, have a profound bias toward the natural style. To be sure, these people admire pattern beds in the parks, and they put into their own dooryards the most distastefully unnatural objects conceivable; but this is due to their ignorance of the value of unity and their pure inability to grasp the real motive of a harmonious composition. In general they have a much greater, though unthinking, attachment to noble trees, natural shrubberies, green lawns and cool shadows, or to a pleasant combination of all these elements.

PUBLIC PARK DEVELOPED IN THE NATURAL STYLE

GAINING NATURALNESS

A few simple rules will help to gain this naturalness, which is lost oftener by thoughtlessness than by intention. Perhaps it is not strictly correct to say that naturalness is gained. As a matter of fact, when a house is built or a park laid out naturalness is lost to some extent. But by thoughtful work we may subtract greatly from the artificiality of the construction, and in that sense it is true that naturalness is gained.

Open lawns are the natural foundation of a natural landscape. They should be as large and as little interrupted as circumstances will allow. Speaking in a very general way, and with room for exceptions, it is good practice to devote all the center and interior of any landscape piece to open lawn. The plantings of trees and shrubs should, as a rule, be confined to the boundaries. Buildings should be located toward one side. And most certainly should the drives and walks never cut through the middle of the grounds if a natural, rural effect is to be preserved.

These lawns may be kept clipped, or the grass may be allowed to grow at its own will; but clipped lawns have a distinct suggestion of artificiality, and the clipping should be confined to the vicinity of buildings or other positions where smooth surfaces and straight lines are already in evidence. The unmowed lawn is suitable for larger places and for more emphatically natural surroundings. The lawn should cover a comparatively large area. One would not want the furniture in the parlor to take up three-fourths of the room; much less would one want the green carpet of the lawn nearly covered with such furniture as trees and flower beds.

Curved lines are usually natural, but not necessarily so. They may be grotesque and artificial to almost any degree, but it requires an effort to make them bad. Straight lines are specifically unnatural. Nature works only in curves. The planets move in curves, the smallest leaflet is bounded by curves, and your sweetheart's face has not the faintest suggestion of a straight line. You will with great difficulty find a straight line in nature. Inasmuch as the grounds on which the landscape gardener works often exist chiefly for some utilitarian purpose, many strictly non-natural features must be introduced, and in many cases the naturalness of the curved line must be abandoned for the usefulness of the straight. This is sometimes true of walks and drives, which are usually the most conspicuous lines on the grounds; yet the general rule must still be adhered to,—that the drives and walks should be curved unless there is some good reason to the contrary.

But it is not enough that the drives should be curved. There are good curves and bad ones, and if a curve is to be used more thought and skill are required to save it from defect than though a straight line had been chosen instead. In an earlier day the imitators of the English style,—not the legitimate practitioners,—in their enthusiasm for curved lines laid out many which were unpleasing to the last degree. The unmethodical, senseless, meandering, serpentine walks which one still sees sometimes are not natural, nor are they artistic in any sense. It is commonly said that every curve in a drive or a walk should have an apparent justification. Thus, if a considerable hill or a group of trees lies within the bend it seems to furnish a reasonable excuse for the curve. Objects which are not manifestly of sufficient importance to demand a turn in the drive are palpably artificial and worse than useless. Thus, a flower bed in the curve of a drive fills the wayfarer with nothing but disgust; for he sees that it might just as well have been put somewhere else and his way shortened by straightening out the wiggle. For any moderate distance a double curve, passing first to one side and then to the other of a straight line, will be often useful. While it departs least from the straight line, it gives the most constant change of direction. It also presents a greater variety of views. It is essentially the "line of beauty." Yet it would never do to repeat this form of curve too frequently. Other combinations must suggest themselves to the designer who has any feeling for outline.

Grouped trees give an appearance of naturalness because, in nature, trees are almost always grouped. At any rate, they are never set in rows! A good, strong oak grows up,—a patriarch of the forest. There soon appears, under the shelter of its spreading branches, a younger generation like unto the parent, and so we have a group of oaks. A group of walnuts arises likewise in another place; and even such trees as the willows and poplars, which distribute seeds far and wide, are found growing grouped together where the environment is specially suited to their development. It ought not to be necessary to argue that this is the only natural way of placing trees and shrubs; yet this most obvious of all rules is too often disregarded.

Shrubs are seldom used too much, and they are frequently neglected. Without stopping to call attention to the wonderful diversity of riches from which we may select when we wish to employ shrubs, (See Chapter XX) we desire now only to point out that their liberal use is in accord with the natural style which we are seeking to develop. Referring again to nature, we find shrubs distributed all about her woodland, and especially along the borders of her woods. Since at best we seldom have more than a woodland border in our garden compositions, its embellishment with shrubs becomes an oft-recurrent problem. A judicious arrangement of shrubbery will often obliterate more of the unpleasant, unnatural and inartistic features of the grounds than any amount of other material or other work. Shrubs may be used in comparative profusion, because they take up but little room. A good view of some things can be obtained over the tops of low shrubs, and they can thus be given positions quite forbidden to trees.

The union of the buildings with the grounds, so that the former seem parts of the latter, is also oftenest effected by the use of shrubs. A building with its

RESIDENCE GROUNDS IN THE NATURAL STYLE

smooth surfaces and rectangular lines arising abruptly out of the lawn gives a distinct note of disharmony. The remedy is to break up, and, as far as possible, to obliterate the line of demarcation. Shrubs irregularly grouped along the walls and massed in retreating angles help to do this. Their most efficient assistants are the climbers, which may cling to the walls or twine about the porches, becoming almost part and parcel of the building. Shrubs and climbers together, judiciously placed, will often bring into the closest harmony a house and grounds which without them would have been at never-ending war with one another.

LOSING NATURALNESS

It is not a very logical arrangement of the subject which classifies topics under these two exactly opposite heads,—gaining naturalness and losing naturalness. And yet it has the advantage of convenience. For it is convenient to consider some things as excellencies and some others as faults, some as commissions and some as omissions, some positively and others negatively; and it may not be amiss to mention certain very important matters from both sides.

Thus, of the prominent lines of the ideal landscape we have said that, other things permitting, they should be curved; and yet there is no redundancy in saying here that they should not be straight. The doctrine is of sufficient importance to merit a second mention. In reality it is often disregarded, to the great detriment of gardens, public parks and house grounds. Yet others make a mistake by accepting it too exclusively, and laying curves where there is no room for them and sending the wayfarer a long journey for which he has neither heart nor time. Straight lines must sometimes be used, but the gardener must then content himself that naturalness is lost.

Artificial constructions, in the sense here used, is meant to cover a multitude of whims and fancies which small gardeners—and some of higher rating—are always introducing in their choicest and most conspicuous places. Frequently these are of the most puerile order; sometimes they are very disgusting. As instances come under my own observation, I may mention a lawn vase made of an old stove painted red; a big rat-trap trellis with no honeysuckles to grow on it; a pile of oyster shells supporting a plant tub on the green lawn; and small flower beds edged with inverted beer bottles.

One of the most generally distributed mistakes of this sort is the conventional rockery. There is not space here to explain how to make a good rockery; but the general principle needs most to be emphasized, that nothing will save a rockery from condemnation unless it appears natural to its surroundings. It may be added that the proper surroundings are not easily secured; and that the small, flat front yard of a city lot can never furnish the associations to justify a rockery. When a heap of stones is dumped in the middle of the hand's-breadth of clipped lawn it must be evident to the most sightless observer that naturalness is lost.

Another affair much affected in some places is the little trellis placed on the lawn for the exhibition of climbing plants. This gives always a note of discord amidst natural or semi-natural elements, and it is very doubtful if such a trellis could be made agreeable in any method of gardening. Climbers on the porches and walls or on old tree trunks, or clambering freely over the tops of bushes, give a more efficient expression of naturalness than almost any other material at the command of the horticulturist; and it is perhaps because of this that they break so forcibly upon the quietness of the scene when treated improperly.

The summer house, which may also be one of the choicest charms of certain grounds, sometimes appears as a very monster of ugliness. A long chapter might be written here, also, detailing what is good and what bad in the way of summer houses, rustic arbors and shady garden seats, but it answers better our present purpose to observe that these are points at which naturalness is often lost, and which, therefore, require careful treatment and good taste to adapt them quite to the best interests of a whole, natural composition.

Bad fences are worthy of separate mention. And the first thing to be said is that practically all fences are bad, considered merely as items in a garden composition in the natural style. Yet there are wonderful degrees of badness among fences. Good, well kept horticultural hedges of privets, roses, spiræas, diervillas, arbor vitæs, and other plants suitable for the special purposes in view, are at least bearable, and are sometimes distinctly satisfactory. A hedge may be continuous and yet irregular, broadening in one place, bending in another, and further along merging into a larger group of trees and shrubs. In this way it

VERY NATURALISTIC PICTURE ON A COLLEGE CAMPUS

may serve the purposes of a fence without marring the naturalness sought. But what shall we say of the picket and great board fences which once embraced so many otherwise decent private and public plots? What shall we say to this frenzy of iron work which stands between us and the grounds we would so gladly admire? Plainly naturalness is lost,—utterly and irrecoverably lost. These fences serve a purpose. They answer to a want keen and urgent in the ordinary home-owner's heart; that is, to the desire for seclusion and privacy and the unmolested and unobserved enjoyment of the owner's home surroundings. This seclusion is worth striving for in the garden plan; but if naturalness is desired, some other expedient ought to be worked out compatible alike with naturalness and seclusion. It has sometimes been thought worth while to sink the fences in deep ditches, the banks of which were given special treatment to conceal the whole; but this means will not commend itself to many operators; neither is it adapted to many cases.

Pure white is not a color common in nature, and the dazzling reflection from extended white surfaces reveals an artificiality which is glaring in a double sense. Thus while white paint and whitewash have many practical uses, and in appropriate surroundings please the eye, they should be shunned where a strict adherence to the natural style is desired.

There are many unnatural methods of plant training in vogue; and it goes without saying that they are inconsistent with the natural style. Yet we constantly find them intermingled with purely natural objects, to the obvious detriment of both. The junipers, boxes, arbor vitæs and similar plants trimmed into smooth cones, vases, globes and more complex combinations, illustrate this method. Weeping tops grafted on straight, upright trunks belong to the same class. Others might be mentioned, some good and some bad in themselves, but all agreeing in the certainty with which they spoil the unity of any place in which informal treatment is essayed.

CHAPTER VIII

THE ARCHITECTURAL STYLE

> The evident harmony of arrangement between the house and surrounding landscape is what first strikes one in Italian landscape architecture,—the design as a whole, including gardens, terraces, groves, and their necessary surroundings and embellishments, it being clear that no one of these component parts was ever considered independently, the architect of the house being also the architect of the garden and the rest of the villa.
>
> *Charles A. Platt.*

A number of terms, all equally clear and useful, have been used for this well-defined style of gardening. We need to notice three,—architectural, formal and Italian. Of these the first is best for our purposes, especially, if architecture is understood in the broadest sense to include all the exterior accessories of buildings, to which the work of the architect may rightfully extend. Columns, obelisks, arches, fountains, statues and groups of statuary, and all similar structures whatsoever, are in this sense included within the common range of architecture and architectural gardening. Indeed, the earliest and some of the best examples of this style were planned and executed by professional architects,—men who did not claim to be gardeners at all. The term "formal" has its obvious signification. It is perfectly legitimate, and in many places highly serviceable. This method is also widely and properly known as the Italian style, having received its best development in Italy.

The architectural style is diametrically opposed at all points to the extreme natural style. It is opposite in methods and in effects; though this is no reason why a person of artistic taste may not find full satisfaction in either. The most modern tendency is to ad-

AN ELABORATE FORMAL GARDEN

mit the architectural, the natural and all other possible styles of gardening, to equal consideration; to recognize that each may claim advantages in special situations; and to choose from among different styles, in a frame of mind quite free from prejudice, the one best suited to any given circumstances of environment and demand. The time was,—and recently,—when English and American gardeners were very much prejudiced against geometrical methods of all sorts. As a result, their attempted naturalistic effects were forced into situations where grievous failure alone could meet them, but where a less partisan good taste might have achieved beautiful and satisfying results through the discredited methods.

Formal gardening has made great progress in America during the last 50 years. It is now better understood, more justly appreciated and much better practiced. The formal gardens more recently made are of better design and are more clearly fitted to their surroundings. It is now seen, in fact, that many small, rectangular plots—as for example within a quadrangle of buildings, or at the side of a residence on a small lot—may be more conveniently treated in simple formal style than in any affected "natural" style. This plain, straightforward sort of formal gardening, in particular, has a real place and is rapidly advancing in popularity.

Before beginning to point out the specific contrivances by which the perfection of the architectural style is sought, it will be best to consider its broader relations, conditions and limitations. The architectural garden is, in a very proper sense, an extension,—a development of the adjoining building or buildings. A dwelling house must have porches, promenades, provision for the exercise, rest or enjoyment of its inhabitants in the open air, with more or less protection under foot and overhead. A public building must have its colonnades, pergolas, loggias and approaches. These may extend indefinitely away from the proper walls of the building and into the area of the garden. It is necessary only to keep up a close and obvious connection between the entrance steps, the walks of stone or marble flagging, the resting seats of hewn stone, the fountains, the statuary and the stone boundary walls, to see how completely the main edifice may extend quite to the boundary of the grounds.

Looking at it in this light it is manifest that the surrounding grounds, developed from the central building, are accessory and subordinate to it. They serve as an appropriate frame in which to exhibit the beauty of the building. They do not attempt to hide the main work of architecture, nor to draw attention away from it, but to point out and emphasize its beauties. It would be well if this point were borne in mind by landscape gardeners in general; for there are many cases in which the buildings are of supreme interest, and any gardening, which openly competes with them for public attention and admiration is intolerable. It is doubtful if any naturalistic effects should ever be attempted in such cases.

The principle of choice between the two great styles has already been pointed out. In situations where the buildings are necessarily predominant, the architectural style is more easy of application, while in those cases where the grounds are naturally of chief importance, they respond most readily and satisfactorily to the natural style of development. This rule may not be proof against exceptions, but it is safe.

One word more needs to be said. A compromise or combination of the two styles, the natural and the architectural, is impracticable and impossible. Certain concessions to architecture are always necessary in natural gardening, even in Yellowstone National Park,

COUNTRY HOUSE WITH FORMAL TERRACE

but they must always be looked upon as detracting from the ideal, and their thoughtless introduction or unskillful treatment may quickly damage the naturalistic landscape beyond repair. And so must flowers, foliage and trees be brought into the architectural garden, but they must, by appropriate methods, be subordinated to the geometrical outlines of the main features.

Geometrical lines, always to be avoided in naturalistic gardening, are to be conservatively sought in working out the architectural ideal. Flower beds, borders, drives, walks, and all other similar elements of the landscape, which in naturalistic compositions would preferably be expressed in flowing curves, will in this style be set in straight lines and geometrical curves. There are pleasing geometrical lines, and unpleasing ones. More exactly are there good combinations of geometrical lines, and bad ones. To discriminate between the good and the bad requires the same taste that is needed to criticize any other art object. To originate a good one in the imagination and successfully to transfer it to the garden requires the mind and the education of an artist.

The amateur may remember that these three tests can safely be applied to his geometrical lines: Simplicity, boldness, grace. Simplicity is of supreme importance. Intricate or complex geometrical designs, which do not appear at once clear and reasonable, even at the first careless, inattentive glance, are curiosities fit for intellectual study, and not elements of a picture for the delight of the more subtle esthetic faculties. They might serve a purpose in a museum. In a garden they have no place. This is especially to be insisted on at this point, for the novice can easily combine geometrical forms; but doing so without training and without sympathy, his work is at best grotesque, and quite apt to be silly. This same lack of feeling for dignity of outline results in tameness, weakness, puerility, in place of that quality which we have designated as boldness. We might have called this quality dignity; but dignity is both simple and bold. Now if simplicity and boldness alone were demanded of geometrical lines, perfection would be within easy reach. One would have only to confine himself to rectangular combinations to achieve both. But some more graceful outlines are desired by the eye, and to their invention the designer may well give earnest study.

The lawn has already been referred to as being in a double sense the groundwork of the garden picture. The close shaven lawn is the very life of the architectural garden. Often it is all the garden there is. If a city residence crowds upon a busy street, trees, shrubs and flowers are all impracticable; but the little strip of close cut grass between is clean, cool and comfortable. A court yard may be chiefly concerned with a fountain, stone flagging and heavy benches; but there may be some little patches of clipped grass in between, and these will be like the carpets within the building. The uncut lawn with grass running riot is so evidently out of unity with all architectonic features as to need no remark.

Trees set in rows may or may not add to the perfection of the Italian style. If trees are to be used in any moderate number they should usually stand in rows; and if they approach closely to some extended geometrical line they should always be placed parallel to it. This applies to those infrequent instances in which a row of trees will appear next the long face of a build-

A GOOD AMERICAN EXAMPLE OF FORMAL GARDENING

ing, and to the more common cases in which they will follow a drive or walk. It is quite the delight of the landscape architect to form long avenues of stately trees; and how successful such leafy avenues have been in satisfying the longings of men's hearts one need only consult the historian, the story writer and the poet to learn.

Street planting should be referred, for discussion, to this place in our outline; and it is a matter of such general importance, and yet one in which such a surprising amount of bad taste is displayed, that we may give it a proportionally large amount of our attention. The street, then, is to be regarded as a geometrical figure, and is to be consistently treated as such. This requires three things. First, the rows should be parallel with the street. Second, the trees should be set at uniform distances. Third, the individual trees should be just as nearly uniform in all respects as it is possible to make them. The first two considerations are sufficiently obvious. The third rule is constantly violated. It is not at all uncommon to find two or more distinct species mixed together in the same row. The writer remembers to have seen nine different species in a single row running only half the length of a city block. This row was purposely set in such an order by the enthusiastic owner of the property. The man might consistently have sewed nine monstrously different buttons in a row down the front of his Prince Albert coat.

Great effort should further be made to have all the

trees in any given row of the same size and form. If in the first planting of a street only a part of the trees grow, no time or pains can be spared quickly to fill the vacancies. And during the early development of the row attention should be given to favor the slow growing specimens and to check the strong. After a row of trees of a single species is well started, a satisfactory uniformity will usually result without further special attention. It is, of course, not desirable to try to make each elm tree along an avenue the exact counterpart of some model; but with trees of more precise forms even this effort is worth while. There are some species of trees having forms almost architectural in themselves, such as the Lombardy poplar; and for purely ornamental purposes such trees may be used with marked success along avenues. Other trees, as arbor vitæs, which can be clipped into distinctly geometrical forms, might undoubtedly be used with abundant satisfaction in certain cases for the same purposes.

Clipped trees and shrubs are frequently seen in the little gardens about our city and country residences. But among the numerous specimens of this sort which one sees, it is hard indeed to find one which really adds some value to the scene. They are usually mere freaks of the gardeners' imagination. They should be severely discouraged. But in a consistently developed Italian garden, judiciously placed among harmonious surroundings, these clipped plants may become beautiful, even dignified. The clipped hedges of the Italian villas are a most delightful part of the composition. In some of these, sculptured columns are set at regular distances, fitting snugly into the mass of the hedge plants; and thus the architectural effect is accented and improved.

Topiary work was extremely fashionable among the gardeners of England and the continent in the years preceding the development of the natural style. It was more used there than in Italy, and without the related features of the Italian style. Topiary work consists in the clipping of trees or shrubs into more elaborate architectural or statuesque forms, such as to make whole arbors, statues, and often ingeniously grotesque figures. If it is useful anywhere it may be brought into the architectural garden; but its extravagances are always unpleasant, and are now haply out of vogue.

The introduction of stairways, balustrades, urns, fountains and statues in a much-frequented garden, supposing the articles to be in themselves pleasing, must always be a satisfaction to persons of taste. The eye delights in them all. So that when we have quite laid aside the attempt to deceive the senses into a feeling of rural solitude, and are working along professedly artificial lines, nothing gives greater pleasure than well-executed and well-disposed architectural and sculpturesque features. This proposition needs no argument or explanation. It is self-evident, but none the less pregnant for its obviousness.

The colors which seem most compatible with architectural gardening are the deep green monotones in the clipped walls and columns. A mixture of colors

FORMAL TREATMENT OF PUBLIC GROUNDS—GERMANY

in these would spoil forever their dignity and repose. A spotted wall or a variegated column would be an absurdity. But sharp contrasts are in some places also useful, as in the practice of setting white marble statues against walls of the darkest green. For the blossoming plants which are sometimes used in beds or pots, bright and contrasting colors are to be chosen. This practice is also entirely the opposite of that employed in the natural style, where the more delicate gradations of greens and grays are contrived.

A terrace always presents two or three parallel lines, according to its construction. These should be exactly parallel and geometrical in outline. They are in any case purely formal, geometrical, architectural; and they fit easily into an architectural composition and measurably enhance its effect.

Fountains are always appropriate to the style of gardening here under consideration. But limited stretches of still water, bound in by stone steps, walls or curbs, also serve to beautify the scene while still further heightening the effect which we are now seeking. The free use of water pieces in gardens was a chief tenet of the Moorish, Persian and Indian gardeners, and may be said to be the principal attraction of so much of their work as remains to the present day.

Flower beds were notable features of the old Italian villas. The typical disposition of them was within an enclosure of walls or sheared trees, as already described. Within these environs a large number of small flower beds were laid off in geometrical shapes, edged with low clipped borders of grass or box, and separated by graveled walks. Both hardy perennial plants and flowering annuals were used in these little plots. Outside these gardens, in any suitable position, flowering or foliage plants may be found in pots or boxes. These receptacles may be at the successive posts of a horizontal balustrade; they may surmount the newel posts at the foot of some stairs, or they may flank a path-side garden seat. The lawn vases, such as one sees sometimes on naturalistically treated lawns, may be used in this style with greater freedom.

Pattern bedding should be mentioned here because it does not belong to the architectural ideal, though some people may suppose that it does. Indeed, the pattern beds such as we see so distastefully displayed in our parks, showing in gaudy colei and acalyphas the day of the week, a map of the United States or an ugly ship sailing on dry land,—these things do not belong to any system of landscape gardening. Neither do the trivial little mosaics of echeverias and geraniums which one sees in private dooryards. These things belong in the horticultural museum, along with other oddities and monstrosities. It is not possible to speak of gardening as a fine art until these things are thoroughly forsaken and forgotten.

CHAPTER IX

THE PICTURESQUE STYLE

But regularity can never attain to a great share of beauty and to none of the species called picturesque; a denomination in general expressive of excellence, but which, by being too indiscriminately applied, may be sometimes productive of errors. *Thomas Wheatley.*

Nay, farther, we do not scruple to assert that roughness forms the most essential point of difference between the beautiful and the picturesque. *William Gilpin.*

L'irregularite est l' essence du pittoresque.
Edouard Andre.

This chapter is introduced for two purposes: First to treat of a quality in landscape composition which, if carried out to a considerable extent, produces a style really different from either of those already treated; and, second, to represent any number of additional styles of landscape gardening beyond the two generally recognized. There are no common, well defined and well known styles except the natural and the architectural; but there is no essential reason why there should not be. It may even be regarded as desirable that other styles should be introduced and practiced. At present it comes best within the range of our study to call attention to the peculiar quality of picturesqueness; and to suggest that it may, in some situations, be emphasized over a considerable space. In such a case the picturesque is essentially a distinct style. In point of fact it is not very different in general effect from the Japanese style of landscape gardening. But as the true Japanese style is too recondite for our western understanding it will be better for us here to speak

ANDREW JACKSON DOWNING'S IDEA OF THE PICTURESQUE

merely of the picturesque, a term formerly more common in English garden art than at present.

There are many plant forms which are picturesque in themselves, and which may best illustrate the nature of this quality to anyone not clearly understanding what it is. Such forms are those of the gingko tree,

Table Mountain pine, Weeping Norway spruce, Weeping larch, Wier's Cut Leaved maple, the leafless Kentucky coffee tree, and many others. A distinction of a sort used to be made by Andrew Jackson Downing and his comrades by saying that a tree which developed luxuriously and normally was beautiful, while a tree suffering from age and adversity, lightning-struck and wind-blown, was picturesque.

A JAPANESE GARDEN IN CALIFORNIA

A broken and uneven surface is especially adapted to the production of picturesque effects. Indeed, it is not improper, though not strictly correct for all cases, to designate the peculiar beauties of mountain scenery as picturesqueness. Mountain scenery is not commonly architectural in style; neither does it have the smooth and flowing outlines of the English ideal garden. Should a landscape gardener some time find himself with a piece of mountain ground to work upon, he would hardly be excusable should he attempt any other treatment than the picturesque effects usually found in such places.

Even in smaller areas, for example on rocky sloping banks, gardening of the picturesque type may well be undertaken. Here is the true opportunity for the rockery. Here is where rock-loving plants may be grown in perfection—sometimes heat-loving species, in other places water-loving species;—but in any case the characteristic style of the gardening will be picturesque rather than "natural," and it certainly will not be architectural.

Dark color masses and monotones have often a weird and picturesque suggestion for the sympathetic mind. This is even the case when expressed in the formal outlines of the architectural style, but it is more strikingly true when the dark monotones appear in masses of black spruces, or similarly dark foliaged plants. The deep, dark shadows of mountain sides add noticeably to the effectiveness of the scene, and to the quality here considered.

A much broken sky line is not always desirable in other styles of gardening, particularly in the natural. It is, indeed, one of the first points of instruction usually given in attempts to teach the natural style, that the sky line should be broken; but this expedient for variety may well have its limits in most naturalistic compositions. In a development of the picturesque it has practically no limit, and the more the sky line may

A JAPANESE GARDEN IN JAPAN

be serried and cut the more emphatic will be the resulting effect.

The scattering specimens of starved and deformed pines which one sees at some places on rugged hill or mountain sides have a charming picturesqueness in themselves which fits well into their surrroundings. Solid groups of symmetrically developed trees in such situations would be out of key with the general local effect. The scattering individuals have a great pictorial advantage, and such trees are best displayed in middle distances. A single tree is always a middle-ground subject. If it be too close to the observer its composite beauty is unseen; if it be too far, its individuality is blurred. All this is of especial weight in a specimen exhibited for its individual eccentricities. It has even been the practice in some instances to plant dead and blasted trees in pleasure grounds for the picturesqueness of their effect, but the good taste of such a step is very questionable.

PART III

General Problems

CHAPTER X

ENTRANCES, DRIVES AND WALKS

An approach which does not evidently lead to the house, or which does not take the shortest course, cannot be right.

Humphrey Repton.

For an approach to be good there must be an easy turn-in from the high road; the grade within the gate must be as uniform and as gentle as possible; there must be no sharp turns; . . . the house must be well displayed to advancing eyes; and the line of gravel must not so intersect the ground as to interfere with a beautiful arrangement of its parts, or to be itself a disagreeable object when seen from the house.

Mrs. Van Rensselaer.

The great circle of the approach lies beneath the sweeping grasses;
Step lightly down these terraces, they are records of a dream.

Amy Lowell.

The orator takes great pains that his exordium shall be at once a fitting introduction to his oration and calculated to win the favor of his audience. The composer of an opera gives special care to his overture, endeavoring to introduce the best themes of the subsequent score, and to make an agreeable impression on his hearers. In the same way, when a landscape gardener plans a considerable picture he tries to arrange it so that the approaching visitor shall get not only a prejudice in its favor, but also a fair suggestion of its character. Among farmers who try to arrange

A BEAUTIFUL ENTRANCE DRIVE

their homes tastefully, and among people who have summer residences in the country, the importance of an appropriate approach is quite generally felt. In some other lines of work,—park-making, for example, —it is sometimes underestimated.

When the grounds are of any considerable size there ought to be an adequate and more or less defined entrance area. The entrance is of some importance in itself, and other items in its immediate neighborhood may best be made subordinate to it. Usually this area will be more or less enlarged by being recessed from the outside. This emphasizes the entrance, makes it seem more inviting, gives room for a carriage turn, etc. Usually there will be a gateway of some sort; and if the vicinity, outside or inside, is full of buildings, the design of the entrance will probably be architectural in its main features. There is such an infinite variety of architectural ideas to be worked out for such places that no general suggestions can be made.

For country places, where the entrance is made among purely natural surroundings, considerably less of architectural effect is permissible. Some very simple, substantial stone work is usually best. Gardeners of an earlier day, often affected "rustic" work—poles with the bark on—for such places; and though these sometimes give a satisfactory result they are much less in vogue at the present.

It is quite customary to make the turn-in especially on moderate sized places, at right angles with the exterior highway. While this arrangement is often best, it might be greatly improved, in many cases, by substituting a less abrupt turn. The main drive may frequently be arranged to leave the public way more gently at an acute angle.

From the entrance to the house or other main point of interest the drive should proceed as directly as possible, and still be gracefully curved. Its course and direction will be modified chiefly by the contour of the ground. Sharp elevations or despressions must be alike avoided, by carrying the drive around them; but the grade of the drive must be compromised sometimes with the course to be adopted, and nothing will take the place of good judgment in doing this. The curve should be gentle and not winding. It should reveal something new at each turn. The best view of the house should be carefully treated. It own effect should be reserved to it, and not squandered on a half dozen unimpressive and inadequate views. If the drive gives one good view, the poor views ought to be hidden by plantings or by the course of the road.

For very large and stately mansions, or in comparatively small grounds, or where formal design is used, the approach may be straight and lead directly to the front of the main building. Such an arrangement lends dignity to a building which is in itself imposing. Such an avenue of approach is usually planted with rows of trees. Other drives, besides the main approach, may be treated in the same general way as walks.

Walks and subsidiary drives must be provided

where people want to walk or where they expect to drive. But walks and drives are not artistic in themselves. Every foot of walk or drive is a trouble, an expense, and usually a distinct detraction from the beauty of the place. They should, then, be designed to fit the actual demands of traffic about the place. The most practicable thing is often to await the explicit

A PLEASANT AND PRACTICAL WALK

demand for a walk. When a path begins to appear through the grass, the need of a walk is manifest and its general direction pretty accurately indicated.

Gentle curves are better than straight lines, for walks, except upon small places or in a geometrical plan. These curves must be determined by the exercise of good taste and judgment, on the ground. A design made on paper is apt to be unsatisfactory when transferred to the soil unless it is made by an experienced hand from an accurate topographical survey. Even then it may not fit. Curves made up of arcs of circles are not very satisfactory, unless the arcs are comparatively short and judiciously combined. If a road is properly designed, only a short arc will be visible from any point; and this enables the designer, when working on the ground, to make many curves and combinations of curves which would be unpleasing when accurately platted on a map.

PROPER (A) AND IMPROPER (B) ROAD JUNCTION

When a walk or a drive branches, each arm should take such a course as to appear to be the proper continuation of the trunk. Imagine how one arm would look with the other removed. Would it still be complete? Would the whole seem to be the perfectly natural course for the walk? Such bifurcations should not be at too obtuse an angle; and yet this angle of divergence is of quite minor importance if the foregoing consideration is kept fully in mind.

Where several drives or walks meet, upon demand, a suitable concourse must be provided, for at such points there is always apt to be a congestion of traffic.

The size and form of this concourse is determined solely by circumstances. Sometimes such a spot commands some specially fine view. The place may be treated, then, with direct regard to the outlook. When no desirable external view is to be exhibited, the concourse area may have a special treatment of its own. It may be flanked by heavy plantings on part of its circumference, with open vistas left at the most favorable points. Or, if near a building, as is frequently the case, it may be treated as an outlying part of the architect's work, and made to conform to it in shape and ornamentation.

The provision of parking spaces for automobiles is a serious problem in the design of most public grounds, and may not always be disregarded even on small private places. These parking spaces become a part of the traffic system and must be designed along with the roads. When adequate parking space is not provided parking in the roads is certain to follow, and this is in every way unfortunate.

Walks must be well drained, but should not rise above the adjacent soil surface. Neither should they be depressed much, if any, below it, except for possible gutters at the edges. The practical construction of walks and drives is a matter of great importance, but it belongs rather to engineering than to landscape gardening, and besides, there is not room here for a discussion of it. The principal artistic demands have, however, been pointed out.

CHAPTER XI

THE PLANTING OF STREETS

> The villages of New England, looking at their sylvan charms, are as beautiful as any in the world. Their architecture is simple and unpretending,—often, indeed, meager and unworthy of notice. The houses are surrounded by inclosures full of trees and shrubs, with space enough to afford comfort, and ornament enough to denote taste. But the main street of the village is an avenue of elms, positively delightful to behold. Always wide, the overreaching boughs form an aisle more grand and beautiful than that of any old Gothic cathedral. *Andrew Jackson Downing.*

We have already alluded to the treatment of streets, saying that streets and avenues, since they manifestly follow geometrical lines, demand a formal treatment. And this formality ought to go further than the mere alignment of the trees. It is still more important that the various trees should be of the same species and of the same age and uniformly developed. Not enough pains is commonly taken to secure these desiderata. One can easily satisfy himself by his own observations anywhere in the United States that, while street trees are nearly always planted in orderly rows, it is the somewhat rare exception to find a row of really good and uniform specimens. Such uniformity is not easy to secure, especially when its importance is not understood at the outset. The only advice which can be given is to exercise great care in planting and the

SUGAR MAPLES ALONG A NEW ENGLAND HIGHWAY

utmost vigilance during the early years of development.

An explanation of frequent cases of unsatisfactory growth of young street trees is to be sought in the inadequate feeding given them. If they grow close to the street on one side and to a paved walk or row of buildings on the other, their roots must of course spread for many feet underneath these surface obstructions. Aside from this the soil is apt to be of the poorest. It is hardly to be expected, in such circumstances, that a thrifty growth can be secured without something being done to offset these drawbacks. Liberal supplies of fertilizers, especially nitrates, ought to be worked into the soil whenever the surface is accessible.

It is a good plan to set street trees rather close together in the beginning, and to thin them as they grow and begin to crowd. This plan, however, demands very conscientious attention to the thinning, for sometimes it is a matter of considerable heroism to cut out strong, thrifty trees along the avenue when they are only beginning to crowd their neighbors just a little. But any procrastination is sure to damage the survivors very seriously.

The distance between trees in the row will be influenced somewhat by the width of the street. In a wide street, where there is room enough for the full development of each tree, they will be planted farther apart. If the street is wide enough, the trees should always stand between the walk and the curb. It is wide enough if, from curb to curb, the width is one and a half times the distance recommended for the trees in the rows. On a narrower street, trees should stand between the walk and the buildings or should be dispensed with. There are many beautiful streets in this country which support four rows of trees. Such streets should have the central avenue twice as wide as the distance between trees in the row; and the distance between the two rows on either side should be somewhat less than that between trees.

There should also be considered the case of quite narrow city streets where there is not room enough for a double row of trees. Here it may be possible to have a single row, perhaps on the northern—the sunnier—side of the street; and this expedient is worth careful consideration in many cases.

If, now, we are seeking a formal effect in our rows of street trees, it follows that this effect will be emphasized by trees which naturally assume somewhat formal shapes. It will not do to press this point too far, but it should have careful thought. We have all seen strikingly beautiful rows of the very formal Lombardy poplar, and the effect of dignity given by an avenue of palms leaves an impression not to be forgotten.

The American elm is doubtless the commonest street tree in this country. It has many undeniably good qualities to recommend it. Over a wide range of country it thrives, but is best adapted to large streets or to village conditions. And yet there are serious objections to the elm as a street tree, besides the fact that it is often defoliated by caterpillars of various species, as, indeed, are many other trees. The elm varies greatly in size and form, and it is almost impossible to find a long street of old elms which does not suffer from the sad lack of uniformity which this variability introduces. The elm is, also, one of the least formal of our trees, and so detracts from the unity of the geometrical idea in street planting. It would be silly to advise planters to discard the elm altogether; but it will not be too much to suggest that some other species should always be duly considered.

The maples are excellent street trees, especially the sugar maple, and many admirable examples of their effectiveness are to be found in the northern states. The sugar maple is a strong, healthy grower, with a regular, clear-cut outline, and has the advantage of a very tidy appearance through the winter months. In southwestern states the soft maple, or silver maple, takes the place of the sugar maple, but is not so good a tree, by far. The Norway maple is suitable for planting in narrow streets, and as it withstands the rigors of city life rather sturdily, it is a favorite with city foresters and real estate developers.

The oaks are better adapted to street planting than is popularly understood. The pin oak is especially at home in decent streets, even well into the city. It makes fairly rapid growth, it has a fine form, its foliage is distinctive and beautiful, its autumn coloring is superb, so that altogether it deserves the vogue which it has of late achieved. Other oaks, as the red and the scarlet oak, are sometimes planted with good effect; and no one who has seen the grand live oaks of New Orleans or Charleston can ever forget their beauty.

The sycamore is a good street tree, the Oriental species being better than the American. The former is sturdy, clean and pretty, with a rather dignified formal quality which suits it well to average street

PALMS FOR THE STREETS OF LOS ANGELES

conditions. The American species is a larger and less formal tree, but makes a good showing in broad village streets.

Other species which are sometimes used with happy results are honey locust, Kentucky coffee tree, pines and spruces. There is a most striking and beautiful avenue of ginkgo trees in Washington leading to the Department of Agriculture; and there are some pretty rows of ailanthus about the Temple square in Salt

Lake City. Poplars, like the cottonwood and the Carolina poplar are used in the trans-Mississippi states, but they are usually a makeshift. It is always very gratifying to find a good street of trees of an unusual species, and this is a thing which the street makers might well hold in remembrance.

Coniferous species, such as pines and spruces, make fine avenues where they can be well grown; but unfortunately there are few circumstances in which they will succeed. Only in fairly rural parks, away from dust and factory smoke, on country estates, or on specially favorable country highways, can plantings of these species be undertaken with any confidence.

Rather strangely it happens that California, Florida and the extreme southern states generally, find it more difficult than the central and northern states to grow really effective avenues of good trees. Suitable species seem to be wanting. Eucalyptus and cypress do well along irrigation ditches in rural places. Pepper trees are used in more cramped city streets, but they are by no means free from objection. The black accacia makes a very good effect when well grown. Of course palms are sometimes used, but they are seldom satisfactory and are not much planted for street use by experienced gardeners.

CHAPTER XII

LAWNS

The star-enchanted song falls through the air
From lawn to lawn down terraces of sound.
Harold Monro.

Turf is peculiarly English, and no turf is more delightful than that of our downs—delightful to ride on, to sit on, to walk on. *Sir John Lubbock.*

It has already been remarked that the lawn is, in a double sense, the foundation of the garden. There are countries, as is generally known, where lawns do not flourish, and there are paved courtyards where grass is impossible; but the practically universal demand for lawns is no more than proved by such exceptions.

The first problem in lawn making is to shape the ground. Some lawns show sweet, gentle flowing curves; others are lumpy and ugly. The designing and grading of lawns is very much of an art.

Where large areas are involved, as on golf grounds, country clubs, large estates or parks, it is desirable to begin with an accurate topographic survey and proceed with a careful design on paper. This design is afterward surveyed back to the land, grade-stakes set, and the operations are governed by the design. On smaller places it is safe to trust to the eye, particularly to an experienced eye. But even an experienced gardener will be assisted by setting stakes, stretching white twine strings or otherwise checking up on his imagined grades. Finally minor corrections, not necessarily unimportant, may be made while the grading is in progress.

These grading operations must keep in view an-

LAWN PANEL IN A SMALL HOME GARDEN

other objective besides that of shaping the surface; they must provide a substratum in which grass will really grow. This implies a good layer of loam or topsoil, mixed with manure, on top. This layer should usually be at least 16 inches thick. If the subsoil is good, with some fertility and adequate drainage, the top layer may be skimped somewhat; but where the lower strata are mainly hard clay, sand, cinders or tin cans, a top layer of more than 16 inches is required.

While the grading is being done is the time to manage the drainage. Open, gravelly soils need no special help, but retentive clays should be underlaid with a generous system of tile drains.

To get a good turf of desirable grasses requires a detailed attention to weather and to the seasons of the year. This is so much of a local matter, conditions in different neighborhoods differing so materially, that it is wise for the novice to consult the town oracle. There should be at least one man in every community who knows all about sowing grass seed.

Generally speaking there are two seeding seasons, early spring and late summer. It is to be observed, further that heavy seeding is usually desirable; also that only the best seed should be sown, even though the price seems rather high. Poor grass seed, mixed with good weed seeds, is about the most troublesome beginning a lawn can possibly have.

The selection of species for the lawn grass is rather a complicated matter. In some sections only bluegrass can be considered; in others bluegrass is tabu. On limestone or alkaline soils bluegrass, rye grasses and meadow fescue are apt to thrive best. On acid soils, however, it will be well to choose bent grasses, sheeps fescue or red fescue. Sandy soils will give best results when sown with the fescues; heavy clay soils are better in bluegrass. Wet soils should be planted with redtop and meadow fescue, while dry soils prefer sheeps fescue. Lawns near the sea, which are apt to be sandy, may be treated to redtop, creeping bent and Rhode Island bent grass.

Lime has often been recommended as a dressing for lawns. Its value is more than questionable, unless one wishes especially to encourage bluegrass and white clover. Frequent top dressings with clean garden loam

A NATURALISTIC LAWN WITH GOOD SHADOWS

or well-rotted compost will serve much better. The best fertilizers are those bearing nitrogen, such as stable manure, nitrate of soda, sulphate of ammonia, tankage, dried blood and sheep manure.

A great part of keeping a lawn in good condition lies in the mowing. A lawn should be mowed regularly, depending on its growth rather than on the calendar, and it is better not to cut too closely. The mowings should be raked off if best results are expected.

Finally it may be observed that in order to realize the fullest pictorial value from a garden lawn it is necessary to limit it to a comparatively small and enclosed space. A lawn which fades away in the horizon lacks intimacy and interest. Also there ought to be some good trees—not too many—placed where their shadows will fall across the shaven grass. The play of light and shadow is the very life of the lawn picture. The shadows look cool and refreshing; but the sunshine is necessary, too. Moreover the shadows on the grass reveal, much more clearly than anything else can, the graceful shapings of the lawn surface.

CHAPTER XIII

WATER AND ITS TREATMENT

> The water surfaces of a park need more study and care to make them appear natural in outline than does the general ground surface of the park. *John C. Olmsted.*

> Urweltlieder sind es, die jedem Röhrbrunnen entsteigen, die Stimme des Meeres der grossen Mutter lebt in dem kleinen Wasserstrahl, wie ein fernes Echo. Menschenseele, wie gleichst du dem Wasser! Jeder Brunnen schliesst ein solches Symbol.
> *Willy Lange.*

The landscape possibilities of any place are almost doubled with the introduction of a fair amount of water surface. Water gardening gives room for almost as rich a variety of plants and plant combinations as does the open ground. There are still ponds, broad reaches of river, trickling brooks, playing fountains, and many other general forms of expression which water may assume; and in each case new opportunities are offered to the plant lover.

The water itself is one of the most effective elements of any picture. A painted landscape is hardly complete without a touch of water somewhere. And a public park would probably be considered seriously deficient without some kind of a lake. The restful and quieting influences of rural scenery are peculiarly enhanced by stretches of still water. The very best effect is gained when the grounds are so fortunately situated as to give

A SMALL POND EFFECTIVELY PLANTED

a good view of a long reach of river, or a broad lake, or of the ocean. This consideration is so cogent as to determine the location of a very large proportion of summer residences. They seem to be gregarious along the seaside and on all the lake shores. This effectiveness of water pictures rests upon a primitive human instinct which has been strengthened rather than impaired by the experiences of civilization. For every reason, then, stress must be laid upon the value of such water views. They must be sought, preserved and sympathetically displayed.

When the point of view is at the water's edge the water forms the entire picture,—excepting, of course, the background of trees or mountains which may be beyond it. But when, as usual, the house, or the path, or the drive is some distance from the shore, the treatment of the intervening foreground becomes a delicate and important matter. The gardener who would plant a coleus bed on the sea beach would properly be sent to the insane asylum; but any other gaudy or trivial piece of work put into the foreground would be as inexcusable. To give the water best effect the space between it and the observer should be obstructed the least possible. Usually it will be in grass. It will be only moderately undulating. A perfectly flat surface and broken ground are equally to be avoided.

The view should then be set off at the sides by large trees, if possible. Nothing else answers quite so well. If they can be arranged so as to be seen in a long and varied perspective, they will be the more satisfactory.

It is impossible to give an exact prescription for the treatment of all such cases, for a good result depends on the tasteful management of delicate details; and yet, in the greater number of these very common water views, the landscape gardener has choice of only a limited number of devices, the principal considerations of which have here been pointed out.

The small pond, comprehended entirely within the grounds under treatment, offers quite another series of problems. If it is large enough to give some pictorial effect, there will naturally be arranged a series of glimpses and completer views from various advantageous points, mostly near its banks. These will, however, be chiefly glimpses, and are to be treated accordingly,—not with the same dignity and seriousness which are given to larger views of larger lakes, though in general the plan of treatment will be a sort of miniature of that already described.

Besides this, the small pond offers wonderful opportunities for planting. Sedges, cat-tails, lotuses, water lilies, alders and many other plants are especially suitable to the banks and shallow water of ponds. Very fine effects can be arranged with them. The outline of a pond may be tastefully broken, so that what would otherwise look like a mere cup in the ground becomes a necessary and integral part of the whole composition. The grass should come down to the water in places. In other parts a fringe of overhanging alders may form the outline. Still further along the sedges and cat-tails may jut far out into the still water. It is hard to spoil such a picture.

If some of the trees along the pond shore are situated so as to cast their reflections upon the water, their effect will be more than doubled. Everyone knows what a pleasing touch such reflections give to a picture. But the trees must not be of the unquiet sort, like some

A FORMAL POOL

of the willows, always shivering and shimmering in the breeze, for the pond must be still and the images on its surface must be still. It is the quietness and peacefulness of such a picture which attract us, and we are very sensitive of even the slightest interference. And yet some of the statelier willows, especially the heavier weeping willows, make excellent pond borders. Ash trees and sycamores, with thorns, and viburnums, and many more such things, enter helpfully into such effects.

The small rivulet does not seem to enjoy the favor which its merits would justify. It cannot become a part of the same sedate and serious pictures which depend so much on large sheets of water; but it has an equal degree of efficiency in its own way. When the landscape approaches that character which André calls "gay," nothing can be more appropriate than the glancing, glimmering, vanishing, changing glimpses of running water in a small brook. Such a brook should be wooded, and among the trees should be loose tangles of vines, shrubbery, brambles and brakes. Rocky impediments in the bed of the brook, if the character of the ground will justify them, give little, tinkling cascades where the sunlight flashes. Here and there a calmer pool may grow some rushes or lily pads. And every turn gives a change of view, and every change of view a new delight.

A good brook offers, indeed, a multitude of opportunities for delightful landscape gardening. It is unfortunate that such opportunities are sometimes wholly neglected.

CHAPTER XIV

THE CITY OR SUBURBAN LOT

Baldness and nakedness round the house is part of a mistaken system. A palace, or even an elegant villa, in a grass-field, appears to me incongruous; yet I have seldom had sufficient influence to correct this common error.

Humphrey Repton.

The fact is, the easiest way to spoil a good lawn is to put a flower bed on it; and the most effective way to show off flowers to least advantage is to plant them in a bed in the greensward. *L. H. Bailey.*

In the planting of city and suburban residence grounds there seems to be the largest field for improvement in this country. One sees in such places more exhibitions of bad taste than anywhere else, to be sure; but such things indicate the willingness and the energy to do something, and taste often improves as work goes on. Those people who own their grounds in the towns and suburban districts are the truest home lovers in the nation; and as a class they have the means, the desire and the taste,—often uneducated in this particular line,—for home improvement. Still there is quite too little done in the way of gardening or of any tasteful amelioration of the grounds.

While the housebuilder gladly puts $5,000 or $50,-000 into his house, he regards $50 to $100 as ample outlay for the improvement of the surrounding grounds. And while he is sure to employ an architect and pay him $100 to $5,000 for planning the house, he does not think of consulting a landscape gardener to design the grades and plantings, but leaves such things to the cheap day laborer who mows the lawn or takes care of the garage. These things make it obvious that

HEAVY FOUNDATION PLANTINGS

the gentle art of gardening has not yet gained a proper appreciation from all those who should be its votaries.

The first great question to be decided, in laying out the grounds of a moderate-sized city home, is whether a fine effect from the street shall be sought or a comfortable outdoor privacy be secured to the residents. On large grounds both these desiderata may be secured; but on small lots one must be sacrificed. The good, old fashioned English style of securing privacy in small places,—a method adopted by many citizens of a former period in America,—is to have a thick, high hedge all along the front. One still occasionally sees such hedges of arbor vitæ, or privet, or mulberry, completely screening the house and grounds from the street. Such an arrangement has its very simple and substantial advantages, and if it is to be adopted there is no further advice to be given, except to choose a thrifty species for the hedge and keep it clean and well pruned.

A practicable modification of this method, but one not often seen, is to plant a somewhat irregular screen of mixed trees and shrubs and herbaceous materials. Such a screen can be arranged in the same general way as an ordinary border planting, except that it will usually face in two directions. This will shield the company on the lawn from the passers along the street, and will, at the same time, give opportunity for the introduction of an indefinite variety of ornamental plants, some of which are visible from the street and some from the house and lawn.

But a great many people do not live much on the lawn, or prefer for other reasons to make the grounds a setting for the house in such a way that the whole shall give the best possible effect from the street. In such cases there come into play all the principles of taste which govern gardening anywhere. As in other gardening operations, unity is most to be regarded. It is often violated to excess. Many city gardens are only aggregations of unrelated and incompatible features picked up here and yonder because they struck the passing fancy of the collector.

A plan should be carefully made and followed. This plan should be upon very simple lines,—the simpler as the grounds are smaller. It is here, more than else-

A SUBURBAN HOME IN LOS ANGELES

where, imperative that the center of the lawn in front of the house be kept open. If the grounds are small, the space will seem to be increased by placing the house at one side and comparatively far from the street. And then, if it may be done without sacrificing the appearance of directness, the front walk may also be carried to one side, leaving the main lawn intact and very much augmented in its apparent extent. The plantings are then made in irregular borders along the sides of the lot and at the back, with more or fewer herbs and shrubs and climbers against the porches and the foundations of the house itself, according to its architectural character. Mistakes specially to be avoided in such a scheme of treatment are formal flower beds in the lawn, detached shrubs, horticultural monstrosities of all sorts, conspicuous edgings along walks, noticeably imperfect specimens of any kind, etc.

So far we have considered the treatment of the city residence lot in accordance with the natural style of gardening. Circumstances are often such as to make a geometrical treatment even more desirable. In fact, the tendency in this country is so strong toward the natural method of planting that many excellent opportunities for fine effects in the opposite method are ignored. The prospective planter of small grounds, who has not yet formed decided preferences for the natural style, is strongly recommended to bring himself to the clearest possible appreciation of the beauties and capabilities of the geometrical style before he commits himself to any particular plan.

In treating the small city lot according to the formal style, the ground is first laid out in purely geometrical lines. There are straight walks, and rectangular or circular areas for grass or plants; and if terraces are necessary, they are laid out so that their lines form a part of the general framework. Then the hedges which are to be clipped, the formal flower beds, and the other accessories of this style of gardening are filled in upon the plan, according to the principles laid down in Chapter VIII.

Special caution must be given the suburban resident and amateur gardener against planting too much of too many things. Everyone knows how easy it is to over-furnish a room, but few realize how much easier it is to over-furnish a lawn. The flower-loving suburban gardener wants everything in the nurseryman's catalog; and such an appetite is a blessing only when properly restrained.

Perhaps it will be an acceptable hint to say that more things may be grown in tasteful arrangement within a small compass by close planting of herbaceous or semi-herbaceous annuals and perennials in irregular borders, than by any system of bedding or nursery crowding such as is commonly practiced on small places. Many diverse sorts of plants thus forced into company give a fine example of the universal struggle for existence, and of the mutual adaptations to which such an encounter gives rise. The nasturtiums will clamber up the strong stems of the sunflowers; the petunias will look out from under the castor beans, and the verbenas from under the petunias; the yellow coreopsis will mingle freely with the blue pentstemons, and over all will tower the hollyhocks, the heleniums and the rudbeckias. Give them plenty of food, an abundance of water, and constant, sympathetic in-

AN OLD SOUTHERN GARDEN—"THE HERMITAGE"

terest, and how they will grow, and what a jolly place it will be! This is where many a successful business man recruits, all summer long, his flagging energies by daily relaxation among his shrubs and flowers and family.

CHAPTER XV

THE IMPROVEMENT OF FARM YARDS

> In addition to planting about the house and other buildings and the wood-lot, the farm has other features that will count in the landscape. Usually, the more or less undulating fields are beautiful. There is beauty in the bare ground, finely pulverized and well prepared to receive the seed for the next crop; in the young green blades, when first seen against the dark earth, and later, when the grown crop waves in the wind, it has something of the charm of a large body of water. The mere mention of wheat, rye, corn, clover, alfalfa and other crops brings to mind something pleasing to look at.
>
> *O. C. Simonds.*

Speaking for the average farm yard, and leaving room for many delightful exceptions, it may be said that the chief improvement is to be sought in cleaning up and putting the place to order. Good order is a fundamental requirement of all art, and especially of landscape gardening.

Good arrangement in the farm buildings is especially to be sought, both for practical convenience and for beauty. This matter is nowadays studied to some profit in farm management; but farm management and landscape gardening ought to go hand and hand in the farm yard. From both points of view a compact, simple geometrical arrangement of the buildings is desired. Placing the principal buildings in a quadrangle gives the simplest possible layout and one which should be adopted in many cases. The residence will stand on the side next the highway, the principal barn back of it, with the other subordinate buildings, attached, semi-detached or quite separate, forming the sides of the rectangle.

Other plans are practicable, and on certain land preferable. The old New England style of placing the buildings in a long row has advantages and some disadvantages. But the scattered, hit-or-miss, planless arrangement, seen everywhere, has no advantage and no excuse.

Everyone must have felt a shock sometime at coming upon a city house in the country. Such houses are, fortunately, rare; but they are not unknown. There will be the house of complicated architecture, with gables, and porticoes and loggias, and porte-cochère; and there will be all the other accompaniments to give a thoroughly urban air to the whole place. And most persons will feel instinctively what an impropriety such a composition presents. The country house must have a thoroughly rural air. The owner has hardly the choice of any other plan. And to give a rural atmosphere some sort of naturalistic treatment of the grounds will be necessary.

This naturalistic treatment, on account of the considerations already hinted at, ought to be on a comparatively large scale. This is usually possible, for the farm can commonly spare whatever room is required for the homestead and its immediate dependencies. In those rather too common cases in which the

AN IMPROVED FARMHOUSE AND YARD IN CONNECTICUT

house and gardens are of mean extent or are crowded into the highway, the trouble has arisen, not through parsimony of room, but simply through thoughtlessness of the needs of the farm home. A farmhouse ought to have plenty of room; and if the grounds have already been laid out so as not to leave ample space, the best thing that can be done is to reconstruct them altogether, or so far as may be necessary to gain a free and roomy farm yard.

A farmhouse ought to be comparatively remote from the road. The distance will vary according to the height of the house, the slope of the land, the taste of the builder, and other circumstances; but the distance ought not to be less than three times the height of the house, or more if the ground slopes upward from the street. If the house is put some distance back into the grounds, as is sometimes very desirable, and has an approach of its own, the main view of the house ought still to be given at a distance something greater than three times the height of the house.

This is not a work on architecture, but it may not be out of place to make a few brief suggestions respecting the farmhouse itself. Generally some very simple plan of architecture is to be preferred. A sharp or much broken roof is especially to be avoided. Porches ought to be wide, and their floors not high from the ground, especially if the place be level. City dwellers affect high porches and second-story balconies for the sake of the privacy they give; but privacy is more easily secured on a farm.

A farm yard without some large shade trees is a very unsatisfactory affair. This needs hardly to be mentioned. The more common evil is an over-indulgence of this craving for shade trees; and there are many houses badly shadowed and shut in, and many yards cramped and crowded by twice or thrice the number of large trees which the place ought to support. The ax is the remedy in such cases. The remedy is, indeed, very hard to apply to trees which have become old friends, but the improvement will be worth all the sorrow which comes with it. The best way of all is to make such thinnings very much earlier in the development of the grounds, and then there is likely to be much less grief in the family.

To produce the rural, naturalistic effect here recommended, there should be a liberal use of shrubs. And for the most part, the common native shrubs of the woods and fields are much superior to the finest exotics. Those things which are so common as to be slightingly passed by are often the very best. Buck-berries, snow berries, elders, dogwoods, wild roses, sumachs, and many others which are always ready to the hand, should be planted in profusion. If they prove to be too thick, they may be thinned out as they grow; but it is very seldom that such a necessity arises. Of course, many of the nurseryman's shrubs are well worth having, and may be added as occasion requires and means permit. And of course such old fashioned plants as lilacs, syringa and spireas should not be omitted.

In connection with shrubs, a great many hardy perennials may be used to advantage. These are more fully discussed in another place. Annual flowering plants are not very useful or appropriate in the ordinary front yard, though they may be grown in any quantity in the side borders if desired. Such flowering plants are usually grown for the blossoms rather than for anything they contribute to the general effect;

A NEW ENGLAND FARM IN WINTER

and their end is then best served if they can be cultivated in a separate garden plot, behind the house or at one side, enclosed somewhere, or in connection with the kitchen garden. In this latter situation they are likely to receive better culture and more fertilizer, and to give correspondingly larger crops of finer blossoms.

A fence about the farm yard is frequently a positive

necessity, but it need not be a whitewashed picket fence neither a sagging barbwire fence. The less conspicuous it be, the better; and some sort of hedge, of arbor vitæ, holly, privet, or similar materials, is much to be preferred.

CHAPTER XVI

THE AMELIORATION OF SCHOOL GROUNDS

> We have an ideal picture, that refreshes our imagination, of common schoolhouses scattered all over our wide country, not wild bedlams which seem to the traveler plague spots on the fair country landscape, but little nests of verdure and beauty; embryo Arcadias, that beget tastes for lovely gardens, neat houses and well-cultivated lands.
>
> *Andrew Jackson Downing.*

It would seem as though the grounds about a school building stood in special need of such means of refinement as trees and shrubs. But we know how often, especially in the cities, they have not the room even for green grass.

But supposing we have one of those fortunate suburban or rural schools, whose founders have had the foresight and the benevolence to reserve for it some more adequate grounds, what can we do in the way of ornamentation? Obviously, fancy gardening with expensive plants is out of the question. Something simple must be undertaken, and usually something inexpensive. If the circumstances of soil and climate and the attendance of the school will permit its maintenance, a good turf is most to be desired. But in many places this will be tramped to pieces; and then some sort of paving ought to be provided,—gravel, or sand or stone.

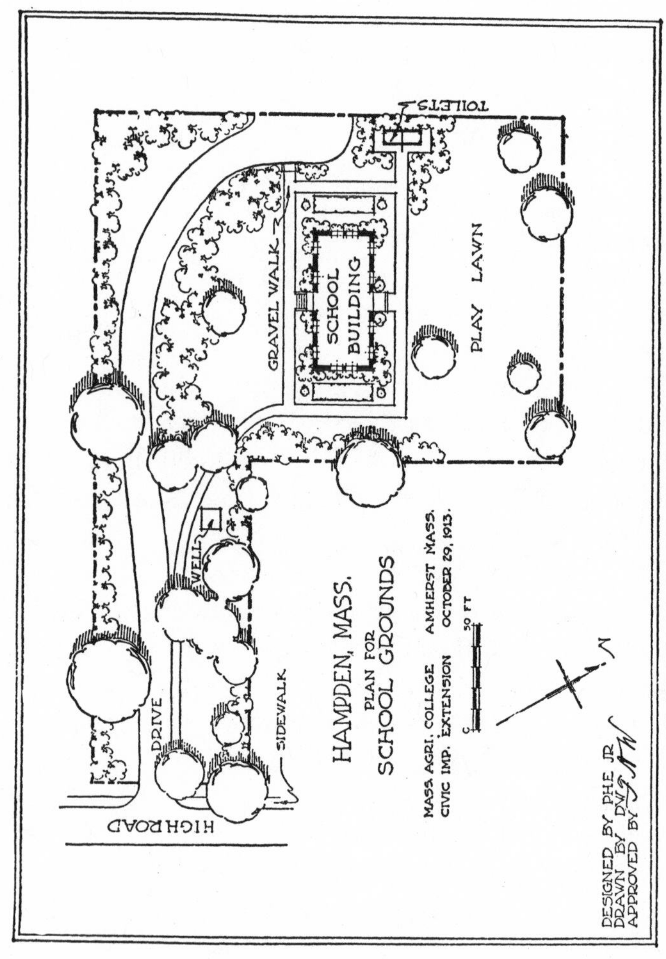

PLAN FOR SCHOOL GROUNDS IMPROVEMENT

If a school yard can have a few large trees they will always be greatly prized by everyone. Their value is so great that, in places having the room, very considerable pains should be taken to supply them. Usually it is best to plant the largest trees possible. Thousands of our American schools celebrate an Arbor day. Usually the trees planted on such occasions are considerable in number, but inconsiderable in size. Most of them succumb to various casualties before the end of term time, and the remainder die of neglect during vacation. If the same work were applied to the planting of one or two large trees,—twelve, fifteen or twenty feet high, with sufficiently good roots,—the chances of success, under the circumstances, would be greater.

Shrubs can be used to advantage on school grounds along back boundaries, especially against fences. Good, thrifty native species, like dogwood, hawthorn, and even the wild bramble, will add greatly to the looks of the premises by relieving them of that cheerless, depressing barrenness which too commonly characterizes the schoolhouse lot. Attention will need be given that such shrubbery borders do not become unsightly by the accumulation of litter, but no other special care or cultivation will be required.

One often hears it argued, how nice and proper it would be to grow flowering plants of economic interest on the school grounds. There is a very sufficient multitude of reasons why this is seldom possible, but the idea is admirable and one to be encouraged. If such good things seem to be within reach, the garden beds will best be put along the back and side borders. It is possible in such stuations, and under favorable conditions, to cultivate narrow beds, laid out in a manner to be out of the way of most of the romping play which occupies the main grounds. But for all such plantings

TIDY SCHOOL GROUNDS—MASSACHUSETTS

the hardy perennials are to be recommended above the annuals, other things being equal.

The great difficulties in the way ought not to deter school boards, teachers and patrons from using their best efforts to ameliorate, as much as possible, the uninviting blankness of the ordinary school grounds, especially in view of the very manifest desirability of such improvement.

CHAPTER XVII

SOMETHING ABOUT PUBLIC PARKS

> One principle should, above all, underlie the art of park design; namely, the creation, from the material in hand, out of the place as it stands, of a concentrated picture having Nature as its poetical ideal; the same principle which, embodied in all other spheres of art, makes of the true work of art a microcosm, a perfect, self-contained world in little.
>
> *Pückler-Muskau.*

> It is a mistake to suppose that the value of charming natural scenery lies wholly in the inducement which it presents to a change of mental occupations, exercise and air-taking. Besides and above this, it acts in a strictly remedial way to enable men to resist the harmful influences of ordinary town life. . . . It is thus a sanative agent of vital importance.
>
> *Frederick Law Olmsted.*

There seems to be a very considerable misapprehension concerning the uses of a public park. In fact, a majority of people would probably say, if pressed to express their true feelings, that, personally, they could do very well without the parks. Parks and public gardens are generally felt to be a luxury, and suitable for the edification chiefly of people of leisure. On second thought, however, anyone must see the error of such views, though it is still very difficult to demonstrate the practical utility of public parks to the skeptic.

First of all, city parks have been likened to lungs, which help to purify the air and so make breathing less hazardous. Those who know how difficult it is in the city to get pure water or pure air will know how real such a benefit is. Perhaps the country visitor, who is used to clean air with plenty of oxygen in it, is most oppressed by the snuffy, dusty, filthy stuff he has to breathe when occasionally he comes to town. But such air is doubtless quite as harmful to those who are accustomed to it as to those who notice it more. It must be regarded as a prolific source of disease. Such air, however, when it has room to circulate, purifies itself with comparative rapidity; and the usefulness of even a small open space may extend to a considerable circumference. The hygienic value of park spaces in considerable.

The public park offers the only outdoor recreation room for very large numbers of city dwellers. This is not the place, nor is it necessary here, to argue that the hurried, worried city population stands in great need of such rest and recreation. It may be regarded as self-evident. One who looks about in any city park on any reasonably fair day will find how large a number of people have felt such a need; and he is much more likely to conclude that hundreds of others should have come to the park, than to think that those whom he sees have no business there. If one thinks about such things while he is in the park and sees the mothers with their babies, the girls and boys picnicking, the young people on their bicycles, the families in automobiles, and the hundreds of others of every age and estate relaxing from the stress of ordinary work, he

QUIET PASTORAL SCENERY IN A HARTFORD (CONN.) PARK

must conclude that these people get some good out of it, which, in the sum total, pays a rich interest on the park investment.

By far the most important purpose which the park serves, however, is that of mental sanitation. The merest novice in city living knows how wearing upon the mind, and upon the nerve centers generally, are the din and hurry and unrest from which no one has immunity. When continually exposed to such conditions, the mind and the senses become dulled and dimmed. The senses need rest and the mind needs renovation. The man who does not bathe his body once a week is not thought respectable; yet no one blames him for letting his intellect go uncleansed for the space of a year. But as the mind responds much more quickly than the body to its environment, it demands the more frequent and thorough restoration. Many minds need thorough ablution,—disinfection. Every mind needs frequent rest and clarification. For these purposes nothing is better than rural scenery, quiet, and clean air. The quiet woodland shade, the cool greensward, the budding and blossoming flowers, have a powerfully refreshing influence which is felt by everyone, but underestimated by most of us. The problem of modern city life seems to be less the development of bodily perfections, than keeping the mind keyed up to the highest point of efficiency; and in the solution of that problem the open park ground must always prove a very important quantity.

If, now, we inquire how the best artistic effect is

to be realized in the development of municipal parks, we have opened a difficult and important question. Under the usual democratic method of management, an artistic success is in the highest degree improbable. We have already familiarized ourselves, in a previous chapter, with the primacy of the demand for unity in landscape composition. We have seen how necessary it is that one mind, free from all extraneous influences, shall create one coherent plan which shall ever after be strictly followed. And yet the ordinary way is to do these things by legislation! Even after a park is fully established in some fair degree of completeness it must still suffer alterations with each change in the board of aldermen.

All this is not meant as an argument against democratic city government, but to point out clearly the tremendous difficulty of securing good landscape gardening in public parks, and to show how imperative it is that every means be taken to secure continuity and stability of park management. There is, of course, no argument to be brought against the demands of "practical politics;" but in those cases, not unknown, where common sense still has a hearing, there is yet hope for an intelligent treatment of this important question. There are places in this country where park superintendents have a fairly satisfactory tenure of office, and where they are allowed to manage, more or less, the development of park plans. There is an increasing tendency to employ competent landscape gardeners in the formation of parks, and other cheering signs combine to color our hope for a steady improvement of park management along with the improvement of public taste.

When we consider the purposes of a public park as set forth above, we will see at once why the natural method of gardening best subserves them, and why

THE PARK AS A PLAYGROUND

they are the better fulfilled the more natural and pronouncedly rural the treatment is. Quietness, restfulness, simplicity, are the most desirable qualities. And this emphasizes the inappropriateness of pattern bedding, of loud color designs, and of all the tricks, intricacies, extravagancies and artificialities which eat up the gardener's time and the city's money, and which, by so much, render the park unfit for its best service. It is said, with considerable truth, by gardeners and others, that the public demand the bright colors and the artificial patterns. Many people feel obliged to cater to this taste, even though they regard it as childish. But it should be said that the disproportionate notice which such objects attract in a public park is not a safe measure of the satisfaction they give. Many visitors are benefited by the fresh grass and the cooling shade who do not notice the lawn and the trees; while those who exclaim most loudly over the wonderful Chinese puzzles in coleus are not helped by them in the smallest degree. Such vociferous features of park ornamentation may be very fairly compared with the crying evils of billboard advertising. When once begun, there is no excess to which either one may not be compelled to go.

CHAPTER XVIII

LANDSCAPE RESERVATIONS

> There are many areas the greatest service of which to the nation is that they shall preserve and display their present natural beauty for the refreshment and inspiration of all future generations. In the case of such natural wonders as the valleys of the Yosemite or the Yellowstone or the falls of Niagara, it is fairly obvious that their landscape beauty is a function not to be destroyed by any other use.
>
> *Henry V. Hubbard.*

When automobiles came in, the park idea, like many others, expanded rapidly. In former times city parks were kept, at least in part, for the preservation of natural scenery where it would be within reach and sight of all citizens. In later times, with greatly improved transportation, practically all citizens are able to go out of the town and visit the landscape where it still remains comparatively untarnished.

This growth of the park idea is indeed curious and perhaps symbolic. At first only little open squares were saved within the city where neighbors could sit in the sun and visit with one another. Then parks were made, still inside the city limits, where grass, trees, water, and flowers made a bright and welcome change from brick walls and asphalt pavements. As time passed the parks grew rapidly larger and more pastoral in their character. Presently the more pro-

HEART OF THE YOSEMITE—NATIONAL PARK

gressive cities began to acquire "county parks," meaning yet larger areas lying further out and kept in still wilder conditions.

But now the demand is for state and national parks; and this demand implies still larger parks with still wilder landscape and fewer of the flower beds, merry-go-rounds and other "improvements" of the old-style city parks. The great system of public landscape reservations now being rapidly built up is in fact something quite different from the city park systems; and the problems raised are also different, whether considered socially or from the standpoint of technical landscape architecture.

Several types of reservations have already been developed. These differ considerably in their legal status and administration, but they all agree in the very essential quality of conserving the native landscape and making it available for public education, health and recreation. In some of them these objects, important as they are, are only incidental; in others they are dominating. It will be well to recapitulate these holdings.

1. *National parks* easily stand first, since they most obviously represent current ideals in the dedication of suitable lands and preeminent scenery to the uses of education and recreation. There are some 25 of these national parks in the United States* with a total area of over 7,000,000 acres; also some twenty in Canada, with

*All these figures are only approximate. As there are changes and additions constantly being made it is impossible to give exact figures except from day to day. Any one who wishes to be accurate in these matters must look up the data freshly at the time they are to be used.

an area of over 60,000,000 acres. The famous parks of quite national importance, such as should be known to every one, are the grand Canyon in Arizona, the Yellowstone with its unmatched geysers in Wyoming, Yosemite in California, and Glacier Park in Montana. In Canada the outstanding national parks are Rocky Mountains Park on the east slope of the Rocky Mountains in Alberta, Yoho Park in British Columbia, Glacier Park at the summit of the Silkirks in British Columbia, and Jasper Park in northern Alberta, 4,400 square miles in area.

2. *National Forests,* both in Canada and the United States, include vast holdings of wild lands. The areas are fairly enormous. In the continental United States there are now 154 of these national forests with an area of approximately 156,000,000 acres, an area about three and a half times the extent of all New England. The Canadian national forests have a present area of over 22,000,000 acres. One single forest, the Rocky Mountain Forest Reserve in the province of Alberta, contains nearly 21,000 square miles. With only minor exceptions these forest lands are in mountain regions, set with lakes and cut by mountain streams, some of them (though unfortunately only a part) covered with splendid timber. These lands, wild and remote, necessarily include also much of the wild game remaining on our devastated continent, and much of the best fishing. Also naturally and necessarily much of the most thrilling landscape. They are, practically considered, large landscape reservations which

may be used in addition to the usual purpose of forestry, for many kinds of valuable recreation. They are in fact visited annually by millions of tourists, campers, hunters, and fishermen.

3. *National Monuments* constitute another type of reservation under federal control. These are comparatively small areas set aside for special purposes, usually to save some historic locality, some prehistoric relics or some natural wonders. The great "petrified forest" of Arizona is one good example; the remarkable cave dwellings and prehistoric community buildings in the Rito de los Frijoles (Bandelier National Monument) is another.

4. *State Parks* are now being rapidly acquired by many of the most progressive states. Michigan has nearly 50 and is finding more every year. Texas has nearly 100. Iowa, New York, and Massachusetts and Connecticut have excellent state park holdings, as have several other states. This movement is now going forward so rapidly that no one can well keep record of it.

5. *State Forests* are also being steadily acquired by a large number of states; and these lands, with rare exceptions, are suitable and available for public recreation. Many of them include landscape areas of outstanding loveliness. At the present time the two leading states in extent and magnificence of state forests are easily New York and Pennsylvania.

6. *Game Preserves* are set aside, either under federal or state control, for the protection of game or fish.

Sometimes it is expected that the game will be forever protected from hunting; other preserves, or "refuges" are maintained for the breeding of game with the intention of producing a surplus for the recreation of hunters. It is a fair question which type produces the more pleasure; for certainly there are thousands of people who delight to visit the perpetual game preserves and see the deer, or buffalo or water fowl undis-

TURKEY RUN STATE PARK, INDIANA

turbed. Thus in any case we have established an area for genuine outdoor recreation.

7. *Historic Reservations.* Almost every state has some small areas preserved on account of their historic associations. Such dedications will naturally increase in number with the passage of years. We need now only notice that a good many of these historic reservations become recreation parks of considerable import-

ance and are visited by hundreds of thousands of persons annually.

These are the principal, though not the only, types of public reservations in the United States and Canada. It will be seen that in the aggregate they are numbered by thousands, that their combined area runs into many millions of acres, and that their public value is beyond all calculation.

What has landscape architecture to do with all these? In fact, a great deal.

If it be the proper function of landscape architecture to make fresh landscapes by human means, certainly the same end can be attained at times much better by preserving the scenery made by the great Architect. The man whose profession it is to create landscape beauty most certainly must love such beauty wherever he finds it. He will seek to protect it, where possible to enhance it, and as far as practicable, to make others love and enjoy it, too.

Quite plainly it is the duty of the landscape architect (and of every other patriotic citizen) to promote these ends: First, to secure the reservation of many and large areas of natural unspoiled landscape for public use in perpetuity. Second, especially to save great scenic wonders, like the Grand Canyon, Niagara Falls and the California redwoods. Third, to see that these are made genuinely available to all, and to see that they are protected from all unwise exploitation, either commercial or beaucratic.

Besides this common duty the landscape architect

ought to be able to perform one other highly important function, viz., the interpretation of the landscape. The specially trained artist should be able to see more clearly and to feel more keenly than the average man the subtle beauties of mountain, forest and sky; and in some way he ought to help these average men and women to see and understand and enjoy more than they could without the help of the artist. All great art is interpretive. The greatest actors interpret Shakespeare, and the greatest musicians interpret Bach and Beethoven. So the transcendent beauties of landscapes require interpretation, and surely this is the calling of the landscape architect.

Constructively the work of landscape architecture is quite different in these great reservations from what it is in ordinary parks. It consists largely in making the landscape accessible. The best scenery must be found, the most superlative views located, and walks, trails or drives so planned as to bring visitors to these best scenes. Sometimes views will be helped by the removal of dead timber or other obstructions. Sometimes a lake will be improved by impounding additional waterflow. But in general the engineering work of the landscape architect in such circumstances will consist in letting the landscape sympathetically alone.

To himself the layman owes another duty, namely to understand and enjoy the glorious landscape preserved for him in these noble parks and forests. For appreciation is something that can be learned. Taste can be improved, in landscape as truly as in literature.

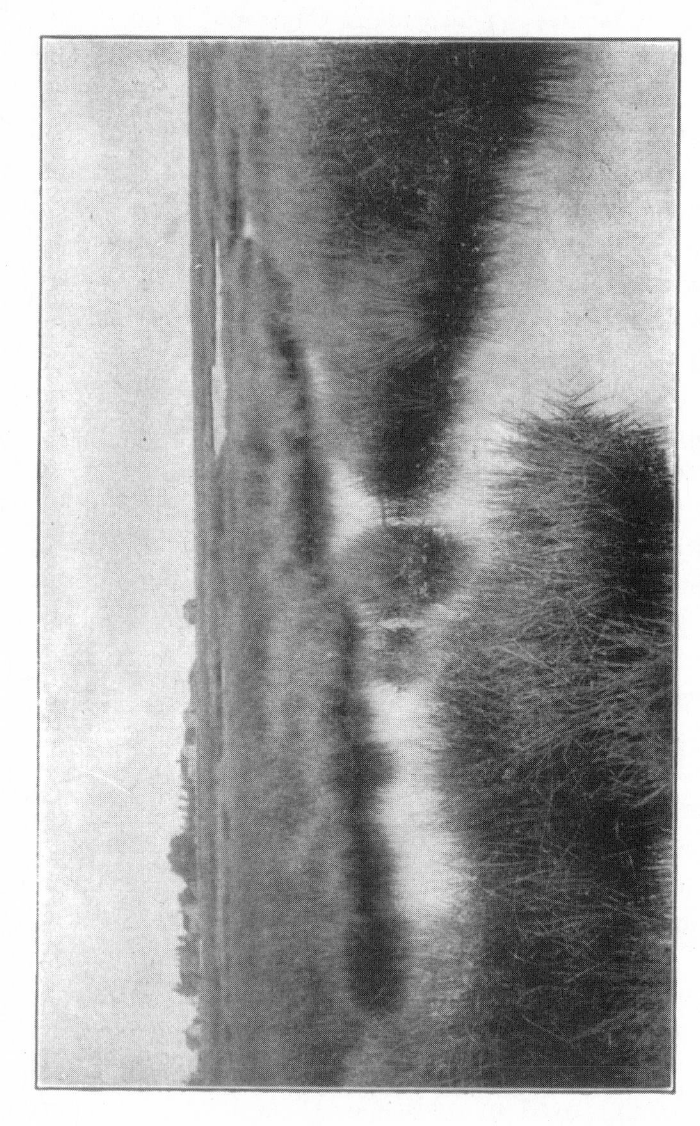

SALT MARSHES—A SKETCH OF BEAUTIFUL NATURAL LANDSCAPE

And simpler than that is the fact that enjoyment increases with experience; the more one sees of such great landscapes the more good one draws from them. It is like the old proverb: "Appetite comes with eating." As one sees more and more of the best landscapes one's appreciation grows.

There is another point here to be considered, and an important one. Most of us do not live in the grand Canyon nor in view of Niagara Falls. A good many of us are denied the opportunity even to visit those famous places. Perhaps we never see them in an entire lifetime. But we do live in some sort of a landscape all the while, and most landscape is beautiful. Some is better than the rest. Our duty and our privilege are to see what is good and to enjoy it. Every one indeed ought to love his native country, to—

> "Love thy rocks and rills,
> Thy woods and templed hills,"

and take a constant and quick joy in the landscape by which he is daily environed. This understanding of the beauty of natural landscape ought to be one of the benefits imparted by landscape gardening.

PART IV

The Gardener's Materials

CHAPTER XIX

A SELECT LIST OF TREES

Many large trees, especially elms, about a house, are a sure indication of family distinction and worth. Any evidence of care bestowed on these trees receives the traveler's respect as for a nobler husbandry than the raising of corn and potatoes.

Henry David Thoreau.

It will not do to be exclusive in our tastes about trees. There is hardly one of them which has not peculiar beauties in some fitting place for it. *Oliver Wendell Holmes.*

In any save the smallest places the trees form the framework of the plantings. They are the first to be considered, and the first to be placed. And unless they are felicitously selected and happily placed and well grown the whole composition is apt to fall to pieces, since it lacks the necessary framework.

Moreover, trees are sometimes able to make a whole landscape by themselves. A forest is always beautiful. And if there are pleasant openings, with long perspectives, and views of wooded hills, or of craggy mountains, or of river, lake or sea, the landscape requires little else to make it satisfying to the most fastidious taste.

Then, too, a tree is a beautiful thing by itself. Each good tree has its own peculiar and sufficient beauties, and even the blasted and storm-torn tree may make a fascinating picture. In all large plantings there should be included a number of specimen trees, so placed as to show their individual good qualities, and so grown as to possess those good qualities in the greatest measure.

For all these reasons the selection of suitable trees becomes one of the landscape gardener's first and most important duties. Familiarity with trees and a sympathetic understanding of their manners and moods is the best basis on which to make this choice; but the following notes, which make no claim to completeness, may be of some service to those who have not made trees a special study.

Apple.—All apple trees are beautiful, probably none more so than the common apple of the orchards. This dignified and highly domestic tree may be planted on lawns and in parks with a free hand. Other kinds, like *Pyrus floribunda, P. sargenti,* and Bechtel's crab are excellent ornamental sorts and worthy of a good place in every domestic plan.

Ash.—There are three or four native species of ash which may usually be collected from the woods or bought from the nurseries. All are good. They are excellent for large masses, and will bear comparatively thick planting.

Beech.—The common American beech is a fine tree where it will succeed. It is not practicable to mass it except in waste places, on hillsides, and the like. An occasional single tree in rich soil makes a specimen to be proud of. The purple-leaved beech is a good tree of its color; but one or two will be enough for a very large place. The fern-leaved beech makes a beautiful specimen, being distinctly better than most curiosities of its kind.

Birch.—Pyramidal and weeping birches have found many buyers during recent years. However, they partake more of the nature of curiosities than of indigenous trees, and are not to be recommended. Nearly all the native forms and species are good in their place, however, in garden planting, though any of them must be sparingly used. The White birch, Canoe birch and Yellow birch deserve special mention.

Catalpa.—*Catalpa speciosa* is the species most planted. It makes a small or moderate sized tree, with large foliage, which is quite ornamental; and the species is further desirable for its fine display of flowers. *Catalpa bignonioides* is a good sort less frequently planted.

Cedar.—The Red cedar, *Juniperus virginiana,* is a fine ornamental evergreen much used in the western states, but scarcely known in some parts of the east. It is suitable for almost every situation where evergreens may be used; it can be massed with fine effect; it has a very attractive color; and other qualities recommend it for more general notice. The Dwarf cedar, *Juniperus communis,* is very effective for planting on rough land and in sunny situations. This and the Swiss cedar, the Irish juniper and other nurserymen's varieties, though they can hardly be called trees, being rather shrubs, are very useful in ornamental planting.

NOBLE TREES OF EUCALYPTUS—SOUTHERN CALIFORNIA

Coffee Tree.—This beautiful ornamental tree, *Gymnocladus canadensis,* makes a good specimen on almost any lawn. Not more than two or three are usually desirable, but they should not be omitted.

Elm.—The American elm is the typical American tree, and the one indispensable street tree. It is, perhaps, the most generally useful ornamental tree we have. No other elm is so good as the common species, though the following are worth using for special purposes; Slippery elm, *Ulmus fulva,* English elm, *U. campestris,* Huntingdon elm, *U. huntingdoni,* Wych elm, *U. montana.*

Eucalyptus.—This genus has so many species that only an expert can remember the names. Several of them have gained great popularity, especially in California. *E. globulus,* the Blue Gum, is doubtless the best known, but *E. viminalis* and *E. robusta* are good species. In fact the eucalypti are valuable ornamental trees, in spite of all possible objections.

Ginkgo.—This strange tree, sometimes called the Maidenhair tree, makes an odd and pretty specimen, but is not suited to grouping. It makes a very good street tree when well grown.

Hackberry.—Sometimes called Nettle tree, *Celtis occidentalis.* This is a good, hardy tree, especially desirable in the western prairie states.

Honey Locust.—This is one of our very best shade and ornamental trees. Its very large thorns, which sometimes prove annoying, may be avoided by securing thornless trees. These thornless trees may be found in almost any nursery.

HORSE-CHESTNUT.—This is a fine tree for small groups. It is not useful in masses, and not at its best in street planting, except that it withstands city conditions well and is therefore useful in narrow streets. For grouping, the Ohio Buckeye or Western horse-chestnut is a good tree of small size.

KOELREUTERIA.—*Koelreuteria paniculata* has found many friends in this country, and may be seen in many parks and private places. It makes a small tree, fifteen to thirty feet high, with feathery pinnate leaves, and pretty yellow blossoms. To be chosen for middle-ground plantings, and used in small numbers.

LINDEN.—The American linden or Basswood is a good park tree, and also good for street planting. It deserves more general use. Some of the European forms are even better.

MAGNOLIAS.—The magnolias seem most in keeping with southern landscapes, but many of them are useful as far north as New York city. Among the best species are *Magnolia conspicua, M. glauca, M. soulangeana, M. macrophylla, M. stellata,* and *M. lennei.*

MAPLES.—This is one of our noblest genera of trees. The common Sugar maple is a typical American tree and one of the most valuable for planting anywhere where it will thrive. In the western states it does not succeed, but is there replaced by the Silver or Soft maple, *Acer dasycarpum.* A fine, semi-weeping variety of this latter species is Wier's Cut-leaved maple, which is especially suitable for specimen planting in grounds of moderate extent. Schwerdler's maple is another fine ornamental variety. The Japanese maples are not hardy in the northern states. Though very satisfactory specimens are sometimes grown as far northward as Massachusetts, they are not generally successful beyond New York, and are at their best in the latitude of Washington. The Norway maple, *Acer platanoides,*

NATIVE RED OAKS BY THE ROADSIDE

makes a fine ornamental, street or shade tree. The Striped maple or moosewood, *Acer pennsylvanicum,* is rather a large shrub than a tree, but is very fine for masses on sloping banks, for small screens, and similar purposes. The Mountain maple, *A. spicatum,* may be used in the same way.

MULBERRY.—The native American mulberry, *Morus rubra,* makes a good tree, and should be oftener chosen for general planting. The Russian mulberry and the Multicaulis mulberry are useful treated as shrubs. They may be worked into thickets and cut back from year to year.

OAK.—The oaks suffer under the imputation of slow-growing. Some species are indeed rather deliberate, but others, like the Pin oak and the Red oak, grow as fast as any good tree. They should be used much more widely for planting in parks and private grounds. Special mention may be given to the American White Oak, *Quercus alba,* Swamp White Oak, *Q. bicolor,* and the Scarlet oak, *Q. coccinea.* A dozen other extremely valuable species may be selected from almost any catalog.

PALMS.—In the extreme southern regions of the United States the palms flourish and make striking pictures in the landscape. Some of them are good for street planting, *Washingtonia robusta* being probably the most popular. The Royal palm makes an effective appeal in any landscape where it can be well grown. In general it seems to be the taste of good landscape gardeners, however, to be rather reticent with their palms.

PAULOWNIA.—This fine tree is seldom seen in perfection. Perhaps it is difficult to grow, though the experience of gardeners generally does not enforce this point. It does fairly well as far north as New York city, where some excellent specimens may be seen in Central Park. At Washington it is perhaps at its best.

PINE.—The genus Pinus contains the best of the

evergreen trees, though for general park planting spruces are more easily managed. The best park pines are the Austrian, the Scotch, the White, *Pinus strobus,* and the Dwarf Mugho. The latter makes a small, round-topped tree six to ten feet high, which is very attractive in certain situations.

PLUMS.—Several of the native plums, particularly *Prunus Americana,* are suitable for more frequent use in general composition.

POPLAR.—Several of the poplars are useful, particularly on account of their easy and rapid growth. They are, however, short-lived, and sometimes objectionable on account of their cottony seeds, which they sow broadcast. The Carolina poplar is a very fast growing variety and useful for quick results. The Lombardy poplar has its own peculiar and obvious role in gardening practice.

SPRUCE.—Next to the pines, the spruces are our finest evergreens, and are, perhaps, even more useful than the former in general ornamental planting. The best are the Norway, White, and Colorado.

SWEET GUM.—This tree is especially suitable to the southern states, where, in artistic effect, it takes the place of the Sugar maple in the north. Where it succeeds well it may be planted in masses of almost any size.

SYCAMORE.—The American sycamore or Plane tree is a striking specimen and may well be used for large mass effects at a distance. It is occasionally used in street planting, and will serve for broad streets in rural villages. The Oriental plane is a much better tree for use in city streets and for park work generally, being more symmetrical and of a general tidy habit.

THORN TREES.—The various species of the genus *Cratægus* make fine additions to lawn plantings, their effect being usually somewhat picturesque. Their small size adapts them to certain positions. Among

WILLOWS EFFECTIVELY USED ON A HOME LAWN

the best native species may be named *Cratægus crus-galli, C. tomentosa,* and *C. coccinea.* The English hawthorn, *C. oxyacantha,* is sometimes planted in this country with fair success.

TULIP TREE, *Liriodendron tulipifera.*—This is a good tree for situations where something large is required. It may be massed in any quantity. Prefers good soil.

WALNUT.—The common Black walnut makes a fine

tree, though it is slow of growth. The Japanese walnuts may sometimes be planted to advantage. The common butternut seldom makes a good tree, but it has characteristic foliage which makes it useful for planting with other trees.

WILLOW.—Many of the willows are useful, especially on low, moist land. The best are Royal willow, *Salix regalis,* the Shining willow, *S. lucida,* the Laurel-leaved willow, *S. laurifolia,* and the Golden willow, *S. vittelina aurea.* The Babylon willow is good in spite of its weeping habit. In general, weeping willows are to be avoided, unless an exception be made for cemeteries.

CHAPTER XX

THE BEST SHRUBS

Deciduous shrubs are, beyond all question, the most important element in planting small grounds.

C. S. Sargent.

If one-tenth the trouble wasted on carpet bedding and other fleeting, though costly, rubbish, had been spent on flowering shrubs, our gardens would be much the better for it. There are no plants so neglected as flowering shrubs.

Wm. Robinson.

The wild shrubs which skirt the waysides have a beauty beyond that of the cultivated exotics in spaded gardens.

Wilson Flagg.

To some unfortunate persons masses and borders of loose-growing shrubbery suggest nothing but neglected roadsides and pasture grounds. The commonness of such materials, and the ease with which unthoughtful persons may pass them by, seem to indicate a certain crudity, if not a real vulgarity, in the bushes and branches. But this feeling is founded upon an untrained sympathy,—upon a true lack of feeling for nature,—upon notions of ornamental planting which are in the highest degree incorrect. There is nothing so crude and vulgar in gardening as an over-display of colors (which are nearly always inharmonious among themselves.) An appetite for these gaudy colors indicates an untrained taste, just as an appetite for dime novels indicates a poor taste in literature, or as a preference for the latest jazz indicates a lack of training in music. The more refined enjoyment aroused by any art are those which arise from delicate colorings, from subtle modulations, from almost imperceptible distinctions. And so the nature-lover delights in the most delicate tones and tints of grays and greens and browns, like those of the pussy willow and the roadside dogwood; and he revels in the beautiful variety of texture offered by the spirea, the sumach and the Judas tree.

We have already called attention to the usefulness of shrubs in naturalistic plantings, and need not repeat what has been said. But shrubs are also indispensable in all other systems of gardening, and a study of the species and varieties at command must be the first business of the gardener. The following list is not at all complete, but is meant to include the hardier and more useful kinds. There are enough for most plantings, for one must not make the mistake of trying to plant everything. A dozen well-selected species give a better effect than two hundred sorts huddled and crowded and jumbled together.

One frequently sees shrubs tied up in straw, or laid down and covered, or otherwise carefully protected for the winter. This has to be done with certain species in certain situations to keep them alive. But there are so many perfectly hardy shrubs, able to withstand everything that comes, that such labor may be entirely avoided. In fact, those plants which have to be coddled through bad weather and favored above their neighbors always give a suggestion of unnaturalness to the place. They seem to be exotic,—foreign to the situation. The perfectly wild garden, able to care for itself and always at home with its surroundings, has a certain permanency and unity of effect which no other garden can have.

Shrubs should be given proper pruning; but they should be spared the sort they often get. Only in very exceptional circumstances should the tops be sheared, or the growth cut back at the extremities. This spoils at once the graceful drooping habit which is separately characteristic of almost every species. When the pruning knife and the shears are to be applied to any shrub, they should usually cut out at the base. Old, straggling stems are cut away, and fresh, clean, vigorous sprouts come up in their places. Many species, like the sumachs, give the best results if they are cut back almost annually quite to the ground, and allowed to sprout afresh from the stools.

ABELIA GRANDIFLORA is a valuable species for general park and lawn planting but is not reliably hardy north of Philadelphia. It has good foliage and better flowers, which keep coming for a long season.

ACANTHOPANAX PENTAPHYLLUM is a very hardy, clean-growing, and satisfactory shrub for mass planting and especially good for hedges. It is a bit thorny, but has many good qualities and no serious defects.

AMALANCHIER CANADENSIS, Juneberry, Shad Bush.

—The dwarf varieties, two to five feet high, are best for planting.

AMORPHA FRUTICOSA, False Indigo. — A good, hardy shrub, though rather weedy. *Amorpha canescens,* Lead plant, is mostly herbaceous, with fine, soft, silvery foliage, and well worth more extensive planting. It has beautiful spikes of deep violet-purple flowers. One to three feet.

APPLE.—There is a considerable list of dwarf crabs of most desirable character which should be considered for lawn and park planting. Their bright and abundant spring bloom and their good foliage recommend them highly. They are not yet abundant in the trade, but may be had from several good specialists. Perhaps *Malus sargenti* and *M. arnoldiana* are the first to be tried.

ARALIA.—This group numbers two or three species of coarse but showy shrubs or small trees. The Devils Walkingstick, *A. spinosa* and the American spikenard, *A. racemosa,* are the best known.

AZALEA.—Very showy brilliant flowers of early spring, and the several hardy native species may be planted freely in all regions where limestone soil does not interfere. The most useful sorts generally are *A. viscosa,* the "Swamp pink," *A. nudiflora,* the Pinxterbloom, *A. vaseyi, A. calendulacea,* the Flame azalea and *A. arborescens*; but many of the other foreign species are worthy of a place in any good collection.

BARBERRY.—Here we have a group of the first importance. Barberries are good for many purposes and are planted every year by millions. The rather dwarf and very hardy Japanese species is the one most used, but the European and the American native sorts are valuable and popular. Moreover there are several other kinds, not so well known, which are altogether good for everyday use.

MASSES OF LILACS—IN THIS INSTANCE SYRINGA VILLOSA

CALYCANTHUS FLORIDUS, Sweet-shrub or Spice Bush.—A small shrub with sweet-scented flowers.

CARAGANA, Pea Tree.—*C. frutescens* is a low shrub, bearing an abundance of bright yellow, pea-like flowers in spring. *C. arborescens* is similar, but larger.

CEPHALANTHUS OCCIDENTALIS, Button Bush.—A hardy native shrub of wide distribution, making a round head; foliage good; flowers white, abundant, in globular heads in spring. Four to eight feet.

CERCIS CANADENSIS, Judas tree, Red bud.—A small tree with pretty bark and fine foliage; covered with red blossoms early in spring before the appearance of leaves.

CHIONANTHUS VIRGINICA, Fringe tree.—A large shrub or small tree, inclined to bear too little foliage, but having an abundance of white blossoms about lilac-flowering time.

CLETHRA ALNIFOLIA, White Alder.—A useful native shrub. Three to ten feet.

CORNUS, DOGWOOD. The dogwoods are among our best shrubs. No one should think of planting a place without them. The native red-branched species, *C. stolonifera* and *C. baileyi*, are especially desirable. *C. paniculata* is also a native species, a good grower, and desirable for its flowers. *C. sericea*, *C. mas*, *C. sanguinea* and *C. florida* are all good.

COTONEASTER.—This genus includes a number of highly useful ornamental species now coming more and more into park and landscape use. The dwarf creeping *C. horizontalis* is specially desirable for rock-work. Other good sorts are *C. divaricata* and *C. integerrima*.

CYDONIA JAPONICA *(Pyrus japonica)*, Japan quince.—Much cultivated in this country. Desirable chiefly on account of its brilliant scarlet flowers in early spring.

DAPHNE.—*D. mezereum* is a deciduous low shrub

with rose-colored flowers; one to three feet. *D. cneorum* is a hardy, evergreen undershrub from Europe, and a great favorite with some planters.

DEUTZIA.—The deutzias are not quite hardy in the north, but can usually be depended on in the middle states, where they are very valuable. There are three useful species: *D. scabra* and *D. gracilis* and *D. lemoinei.*

DIERVILLA FLORIDA, Weigelia.—Included in this species are most of the shrubs sold as *Diervilla rosea, Weigelia alba, etc.* There are many varieties, mostly hardy, good growers and profuse bloomers. The foliage, however, is a trifle coarse.

ELDER.—The common American elder, *Sambucus canadensis,* is a shrub of no mean artistic capabilities. It is fine for massing against trees and along woodland borders, and for working into various compositions. The Golden elder is a showy shrub for use in limited quantity.

ELÆAGNUS, Oleaster.—*E. longipes* has been widely sold in recent years and is a good shrub, with ornamental and edible fruit. *E. argentea* is also planted, but is not so desirable.

EUMONYMUS.—The best species for general planting is the Winged evergreen, *E. alatus.* The Wahoo, *E. atropurpureus* and the European and Japanese species are also sometimes liked.

EXOCHORDA GRANDIFLORA.—A fine shrub, bearing beautiful white blossoms in spring. Deserves more general planting.

FORSYTHIA, Golden-Bell.—One of the very finest shrubs for the latitude of New York and southward, though hardy enough for the milder parts of New England. The weeping species, *Forsythia suspensa* is a great favorite, well adapted to banks and rocky slopes. The upright *F. intermedia* is better for mass planting.

HAMAMELIS.—The common Witch hazel is a highly ornamental shrub, better for wild and rocky banks. Though it is a slow grower and a bit hard to transplant it is worth using.

HYDRANGEA.—Two species are widely used—probably too widely. Both are coarse and excessively showy, but have positive good qualities. The most affected variety is *H. paniculata grandiflora;* but as material for good landscape gardening *H. arborescens* is to be preferred.

HYPERICUM, St. John's Wort.—Small native shrubs of considerable usefulness, of which the best species are *H. kalmianum, H. prolificum* and *H. aureum.*

KERRIA JAPONICA.—A pretty shrub with slender, delicate, bright green twigs, fresh green leaves and handsome yellow flowers. Well worth planting. Three to eight feet.

LILAC (Botanically *Syringa*).—The lilacs are old and never-to-be-forgotten favorites. They are capable of much greater beauty than is usually realized. They should be kept cut back to a reasonable height, the old wood thinned out, and a fresh, vigorous growth kept up by liberal manuring. The fine new varieties, with magnificent large single or double flowers in numerous extremely rich colors, offer a chance for many new experiences with these old favorites. Sometimes the finer varieties may be successfully grafted upon old, established plants which give inferior blossoms.

LONICERA.—The bush honeysuckles offer excellent

RHODODENDRONS IN FULL FLOWER ARE VERY SHOWY

materials for landscape planting. They are hardy, thrifty, floriferous and thoroughly reliable. The best are the Tartarian honeysuckle, the European fly honeysuckle, *L. xylosteum* and the strong and effective *L. morrowi*.

MYRICA GALE, Sweet gale, and *Myrica asplenifolia*, Sweet Fern, are well known, small native shrubs which add very much to certain effects when judiciously set in small masses in the shrubbery border.

PHILADELPHUS, Syringa, Mock Orange.—These shrubs are most remarkable for their abundance of very fragrant white flowers in spring. Like lilacs, they need to be rigorously clipped out to prevent the accumulation of old, unsightly wood. The best plan is to cut all the stems back to the ground at three or four years old, or even at two years old if the growth of new wood justifies it. This keeps up a rotation of fresh, clean shoots. The best species are *P. grandiflorus, P. coronarius* and *P. gordonianus.* Six to ten feet.

POTENTILLA FRUTICOSA, Cinquefoil. — A native shrub with bright yellow flowers. Hardy and inclined to be weedy in some sandy soils. Three to four feet.

PRIVET.—The privets are probably the most popular hedge plants in America and are planted annually by millions. In the southern states the California privet is the favorite, being practically evergreen, but it is not reliably hardy north of Philadelphia and should be superseded by better species. The Japanese *Ligustrum ibota* and the variety *Regelianum* are quite useful for massing and general landscape planting. The Amur privet is probably the hardiest and best for general northern planting, and may well be substituted for the better known *L. vulgare.* All the privets have the good quality of resisting shade and may therefore be planted on the north side of buildings and in other situations where other favorite shrubs fail to live.

RHODODENDRONS.—These magnificent ornamental plants are hardy in most situations and not usually difficult to grow. There are many wonderful and striking varieties offered by the nurserymen, but the beginner will hardly be able to discriminate their merits.

RHUS, Sumach.—The sumachs are mostly very hardy and good ornamental plants. Their spreading, luxuriant pinnate foliage gives a peculiar and somewhat tropical suggestion. In most places they are best if the old growth is constantly cut out and the vigorous young shoots depended on. Their colors in autumn are especially desirable. *Rhus glabra* is probably best, followed by *R. copallina* and *R. typina*. *R. cotinus,* the Smoke tree, is quite different from the others. It is a well known shrub, five to ten feet high, bearing large feathery wands of reddish or purplish abortive blossoms.

ROSES.—Hardy flowering roses are usually best planted in beds by themselves; but many of the native species are remarkably fine if grown in the border with the other shrubbery. *Rosa lucida, R. blanda* and nearly all the native species may be planted. The Sweet Brier and the Prairie rose, *R. setigera,* are among the best. The Japanese rose, *R. rugosa,* is also a very fine shrub for general planting. Many of the popular varieties of the rambler group, and especially the dwarf ramblers, show excellent results when planted as shrubs upon the lawn.

RUBUS ODORATUS.—The flowering raspberry is one

of the most useful and neglected of native shrubs. It should generally be used in small masses for the emphasis which its large, striking foliage gives. Three to five feet. Other brambles are very useful in many places.

SALIX, Willow.—Most of the willows tend to be trees rather than shrubs, but many of them can be grown as shrubs if severely cut back. They are especially desirable for the delicate gray-greens which they give in spring, and some of them for the brightness of their twigs in winter. *Salix vitellina* of horticulturists has beautiful bright golden twigs. *S. lucida* is especially remarkable for its shining foliage. The so-called weeping willows grafted in the top of a straight trunk are to be avoided.

SPIREAS form, on the whole, the finest and most useful group of shrubs we have. Their hardiness, thrift, grace, floriferousness, all recommend them. Probably the best one is the horticulturist's *Spirea van houttei,* sometimes called Bridal Wreath. No grounds anywhere ought to lack this. Then come *S. prunifolia* and *S. hypericifolia.* The former has specially beautiful foliage. The latter is much like a small edition of Van Houtt. *S. thunbergii* is small (one to three feet) and very delicate and graceful in growth and in foliage, but not fully hardy northward.

SYMPHORICARPUS RACEMOSUS, Snowberry. — A good native shrub, with white berries in autumn. Two to five feet. *S. vulgaris,* Coral berry or Indian currant, is very common in the central and western states, and is well worth planting. It is graceful of growth and bears quantities of persistent bright red berries. Two to five feet.

A GOOD MASS OF VIBURNUMS

VIBURNUM OPULUS, Snowball or Guelder rose.—This is a fine, strong-growing shrub giving abundant white blossoms. Other viburnums are also desirable, as *V. plicatum, V. lantanoides, V. tomentosuum, V. dentatum, V. cassanoides,* etc.

CHAPTER XXI

HARDY PERENNIALS

> Now that the treasures of the far East are lavished upon us we have hardy plants suitable for practically every purpose the most exacting gardener can conceive. And whenever we have any special object to accomplish we ought to try nine times to find a hardy plant that will do the work before falling back on a tender one. And this for two reasons: First, hardy plants harmonize better with our climate and environment than tropical plants. Second, as a rule, they are cheaper to maintain. And in the long run, those effects which grow naturally out of the soil and out of true economy will be recognized as the most artistic. *Wilhelm Miller.*

The hardy herbaceous perennials, as a class, are the easiest to manage, the cheapest and the most naturalistic in the effect they give, of all the plants that grow. When once planted they need very little further care, Many of them need none at all, and will thrive and multiply for years in the grass or among the shrubs without the slightest attention. Growing thus at full freedom they give a wild, woodsy air to a place which nothing else can furnish quite so well. Their ability to take care of themselves year after year makes them very cheap. There has been a very healthy and gratifying tendency in recent years toward the more general use of such material, but there is no liklihood that it will soon be overdone.

Hardy perennials may be used in almost any situation where plants are wanted at all. They may grow under the trees, among the shrubs, in rockeries, along the borders of ponds and rivulets, on sloping banks, in borders by themselves, in shade or sun; in fact, it is very hard to go amiss with them unless, indeed, they are put into flower beds. It is a very convenient way to outline a border with herbaceous perennials, among which and in front of which the annuals are planted from year to year. One of the best ways is to mix annuals and perennials together, the annuals each year "taking up the slack" in the border, filling in those areas not yet fully appropriated by the perennials.

Many kinds, especially the best ones, those which thrive, need to be lifted and divided every two or three years. Otherwise they crowd and choke one another. It is also a very good plan to grow some fresh stock from seeds or cuttings or divisions from year to year, thus having new varieties to add to the garden, or at least having fresh young plants in place of old, exhausted ones.

Special selections of varieties should be made for wild gardens, rockeries, ponds and other particular purposes.

Many of the best varieties may be grown readily from seed, but a long list of the very best perennials is carried in stock by hundreds of American nurserymen. They are easy to buy and easy to grow.

It would be entirely impossible, within the limits of this work, to enumerate and describe the most of the good herbaceous perennials. The following list is offered merely as a suggestion to those who are very much unacquainted with such plants. The author has endeavored to select those easiest to grow and of widest usefulness; but as such a selection is a very personal matter anyone else who is acquainted with herbaceous perennials will be likely to choose a somewhat different list.

ACONITUM, Monkshood.—A charming group of plants, though some are poisonous. The best are *A. napellus, A. autumnale* and *A. uncinatum.*

ANCHUSA, a pretty flower of specially clear blue color and therefore desirable for combining with others.

ANEMONE, Wind Flower.—In many species and varieties, all good. Mostly flowering early; usually white, sometimes blue. Among the best are *A. sylvestris, A. nemorosa, A. pennsylvanica, A. patens nuttalliana, A. japonica,* and many horticultural varieties, both double and single.

AQUILEGIA, Columbine.—One of the most valuable groups of hardy plants. Easy to grow from seed. The best species are *A. canadensis, A. cœrulea, A. vulgaris* and *A. chrysantha,* though there are many other fine ones.

ASCLEPIAS contains several good plants, of which *A. tuberosa* is best. It grows in tufts, twelve to eighteen inches high, with large heads of orange blossoms in midsummer.

ASTER.—Several of the asters are hardy perennials, and many are very ornamental. The following deserve

A RICH BORDER OF HARDY PERENNIALS, DELPHINIUMS PREDOMINATING

special mention: *A. levis, A. nova-angliæ, A. novi-belgi, A. cordifolius, A. alpinus, A. ericoides.*

BOCCONIA CORDATA, Plume poppy.—A large, strong growing plant, with large leaves. Fine for emphasis at medium distances. Five to eight feet.

BOLTONIA.—These plants much resemble asters. There are two species, *B. asteroides* with white flowers, and *B. latisquama* with pink flowers.

CAMPANULA, Bluebel, Harebell.—Easy to grow and always attractive. The genus numbers several fine species, such as *C. carpathica, C. media, C. nobilis, C. punctata, C. rotundifolia, C. grandis,* etc.

CHRYSANTHEMUM.—This genus contains several hardy species, some of them known as daisies or marguerites. Probably *C. maximum* is the best, though others are very good.

COREOPSIS.—Fine, free-flowering plants with large, golden blossoms. *C. grandiflora* and *C. lanceolata* are the best of the perennial species. Fine for cut flowers.

DELPHINIUM, Larkspur.—The perennial larkspurs are very showy and valuable plants. They may be had in numerous species and varieties. Those commonly grown are hybrids. The colors in this group are superb, but the best are so far superior to the poorest that great pains should be taken in making selection. As the plants may easily be grown in quantity from seed this process of selection is more pure delight than expense.

DIGITAILS, Foxglove. — Well-known plants of easiest culture, free flowering and always desirable.

HARDY DIANTHUS ON A STONE WALL

The commonest species, with very large flowers in a variety of colors, goes under the doubtful name of *D. gloxiniæflora;* but *D. lantata, D. siberica* and *D. grandiflora* are equally fine.

HELENIUM.—A very fine and striking plant, particularly the variety, *H. autumnale superbum.* Furnishes a dazzling glow of yellow late in summer when flowers are scarce. Six to eight feet.

HELIANTHUS, Sunflower.—Some of the perennial species are very useful in border composition. The best are *H. maximillani* and *orgyalis.* These give very striking, though easy and natural, effects.

HEMEROCALLIS, Day Lily.—This genus, called day lilies, are not lilies at all, but are splendid garden plants just the same. They are hardy and free-flowering, and most of them are of good color and highly ornamental. One of the best is the pale yellow "Lemon lily," *H. flava;* another good sort is *H. dumortieri,* and still another is *H. middendorfi.* There are also a few hybrids worth trying.

HOLLYHOCK.—The old favorite, and one of the most artistically effective plants known. In many colors, single and double. Subject to severe attacks of rust, which sometimes kill the plants. In such cases burn the old plants and all the litter around them and plant anew in a different spot.

LEPACHYS.—A very desirable genus comprising only a few species, of which *L. pinnata* and *L. columnaris* are worth first trial.

LUPINES make a fine show in any good hardy border. There are two varieties of the perennial species, the blue and the white. They appear to advantage together.

OENOTHERA. — Comprises several good species, mostly with large yellow flowers. The best are *O. missouriensis, O. fruticosa major* and *O. fraseri.*

PAPAVER, Poppy.—One of the most delicate and beautiful of hardy plants is the Iceland poppy, *Papaver nudicaule.* Oriental poppy, *P. orientale,* is a large and very showy species.

PENTSTEMON.—This genus numbers several of the best herbaceous plants known to horticulture. They are hardy and easy to manage. Among the best are *P. digitalis, P. grandiflorus, P. pubescens, P. confertus, P. barbatus torreyi, P. acuminatus* and *P. ovatus.* There are several others, and not a poor one among them.

PEONY.—Too well known to need remark. Usually grown alone on the lawn, but much finer when massed in the border against the shrubbery. Propagate by division and allow the plants to remain many years undisturbed.

PHLOX.—The well-known and showy perennial phlox of the gardens is *P. paniculata,* often called *P. decussata,* which has numberless fine varieties. Several of the native species are also very useful for border planting, especially *P. maculata* and *P. divaricata.*

RUDEBECKIA, Coneflower. — Large, strong-growing, hardy plants. The best-known is the variety Golden Glow, which belongs to the species *R. laciniata*. *R. maxima, R. hirta* and *R. newmani* are excellent.

SOLIDAGO, Goldenrod.—A characteristically American genus of incomparable beauty. The only reason people do not plant them extensively is that they grow

PEONY FESTIVA MAXIMA

wild so abundantly. But no garden should be without its masses of goldenrod. The best species for planting are *S. canadensis, S. sempervirens, S. juncea, S. nemoralis* and *S. speciosa*.

SPIREA.—Several of the spireas are herbaceous. They are all useful. The best known are *S. aruncus, S. astilboides, S. palmata* and *S. venusta*.

TRILLIUM.—One of the most beautiful blossoms of early spring. *T. grandiflorum,* bearing large, pure white flowers, is best. Prefers a somewhat shady place.

CHAPTER XXII

THE INDISPENSABLE ANNUALS

The greatest possibilities with color in the garden depend upon the annuals. *F. Schuyler Mathews.*

For the best and most continuous display of flowers during the whole summer season, annual plants are essential.
E. O. Orpet.

The old-fashioned flower gardens were largely made up of annuals. Among flowers, by far the larger part of the old-time favorites were annuals; and it is probable that nine out of ten persons to-day, if asked to mention their favorite flowers (florists' stock excepted), would name annuals. Sweet peas, pansies, asters, cosmos, nasturtiums,—these have a hold on common, everyday people which they will never lose.

And so, while it is possible to find many pleasant gardens,—in snug back yards, or window boxes or tomato cans—without trees and shrubs and perennials, the annuals are omnipresent. Their great variety, their adaptability to all needs and circumstances, the innumerable, characteristically beautiful ways they have of expressing themselves, make them always indispensable.

Almost all of the annuals may be grown successfully by sowing the seeds where the plants are to stand. This is done when the weather is warm enough in spring, and as soon as the soil is in good workable condition. The seed bed should always be thoroughly prepared, with good drainage and an abundance of well-decomposed fertilizer worked in. But it is much the best plan, especially in northern latitudes, wherever it can be done, to start the plants in hotbeds, cold frames, greenhouses, or boxes of earth in the house, from which they are transplanted to the open ground. Considerable time is gained in this way,—often one or two months. Nearly all the annual species may be handled in this way. There are a few exceptions. But many sorts make much better plants by transplanting; and it is often advisable to transplant the seedlings once before they reach their final stations in the grounds.

A common error, in growing annuals, is to plant them in flower beds. This mistake is frequently made with other plants, but never so persistently and disastrously as with phloxes, zinnias, marigolds and their like. If a strictly geometrical scheme is intended, or if the garden is one of the old Italian style, with a high wall about it, then flower beds will fit the place. But in the free and natural door-yard gardening, with which we are most concerned, the whole picture is sadly disfigured when it is cut full of holes to receive strange, detached bunches of unwilling flowers in varied assortment. There they stand about uncomfortably through the summer, each bunch of flowers jealous of its neighbors, all appearing to be afraid of overstepping the circumscribing bricks, stones or oyster shells which hem them in, all chafing at the restraint, and all wishing they were safely away in the woods, where they might clamber down the banks or revel in the grass the way flowers were meant to do. And then when winter comes the empty beds through four months of the year make the lawn look like an abandoned cemetery.

The annual plants ought to be put, not into beds, but into the borders with the perennials and the shrubs. Or if shrubs and perennials are not grown, then the annuals have the border to themselves. Arranged in this way, they are capable of some of the most brilliant and satisfying effects which plants can ever give. In the irregularity and informality of the border it makes no difference if one plant or a whole lot of plants fails to grow. The irregularity is not destroyed! Or if some celandines or dandelions crowd into a half occupied nook somewhere, there is no harm done, for flowers are what we want. It would be different if we wanted flower beds.

The first and easiest and greatest improvement to be made in hundreds of front yards would be to obliterate the flower beds entirely,—sod them over, and leave an open greensward where they have stood in the middle of the lawn,—and move the flowers into the side borders.

It is hardly necessary to describe the principal annuals nor to give directions for their cultivation; but the following partial list, with scattering notes, is ap-

CHINA ASTERS IN MIDSUMMER

pended merely as a suggestion of the manifold riches at command.

Asters.—The annual or "China" asters have been very much improved in recent years. The old-time asters were too stiff and formal to gain much sympathy, but the new sorts, particularly the branching and the chrysanthemum flowering sections, are free and graceful and very fine. The new Japanese asters are also informal and agreeable. The better strains of the German quilled asters are extremely good, and quite different from other varieties. Asters should always be started in a hotbed and transplanted if possible.

Alyssum.—A good old favorite. Works nicely into the edges of the flower border.

Ageratum.—Constant bloomer during summer, in white and bright blue; good in the edges of borders. Six to eighteen inches high.

Antirrhinum, Snapdragon.—Many fine colors, from white nearly to black, in dwarf and standard varieties. To be used mostly in small masses. Six inches to three feet.

Balsams.—Old-time favorites, but not very useful in composition with other plants. They do not transplant well.

Calendula, called Pot Marigold by some.—Thrifty and a constant bloomer, mostly in yellow and orange shades. Ten to eighteen inches.

Campanula, including Canterbury Bells. Some are annual, some are perennial, but the Canterbury Bells are biennial. All are at home in the flower border and are great favorites.

CANDYTUFT.—Good, free flowering, hardy border plant, in several colors, pure white being best.

CENTAUREA, Corn Bottle, Blue Bottle, or Bachelor's Button.—Another old favorite, running mostly to light blues. A new strain of Marguerite centaureas has a better form and more substance to the blossoms.

CELOSIA, including Cockscomb. This group numbers some popular ornamental plants, especially the feathered varieties and those with ornamental foliage.

CLARKIA.—Here is an annual little grown in America but worth while, at least in cool climates—Some of the new selected colors are most pleasing.

COREOPSIS, Calliopsis.—All bright yellows, with unimportant exceptions. Some of the finest flowering plants grown for border or for cut flowers. *C. tinctoria* gives many pretty dwarf varieties, and some with quilled, others with dark maroon, blossoms. One to three feet.

COSMOS.—One of the finest annuals, especially southward. Does not succeed well at the north though the very early varieties will do fairly well. In white and several shades of pink and red. The white blossoms are prettiest. Three to six feet.

DELPHINIUM, Larkspur. The annual varieties are very satisfactory, including soft and pleasing shades of pink, mauve and pale blue. Very easy to grow.

DIANTHUS, Pink.—A good old favorite, and worth

more general cultivation at the present time. Many colors, single and double.

ESCHSCHOLTZIA, California poppy. Does not transplant well; prefers a warm, rather dry garden. Very floriferous with gay and brilliant colors, yellows, orange and scarlet shades predominating.

GAILLARDIA, Blanket flower. The annual varieties need not be forgotten just because the perennial varieties are so popular. All are good, with rich shades of dark yellow and red.

GODETIA.—This hardy annual has been considerably improved by recent breeding and should receive attention in making up the garden list.

HELIANTHUS.—Sunflower; rather coarse, but with bright cheerful blossoms. The annual varieties should be planted in the garden where large mass effects are required without delay.

LUPINE.—There are both annual and perennial species, all good. The annuals are distinctly desirable, in white, rose and different shades of blue; 2 feet tall.

MARVEL OF PERU, the old-time Four-o'clock, is a good husky dependable plant, rather coarse in habit, but a favorite, especially with those who remember grandmother's garden.

MARIGOLDS.—These are of two rather different types, the Double African marigolds, and the dwarf French varieties (Tagetes). Both are most desirable. The African marigolds are large and lusty with an extended flowering season. They bear unlimited quantities of large double flowers in all shades of yellow and orange, many of these shades being refined and pleasing. They grow from 3 to 4 feet high. The dwarf varieties show colors of yellow and red, sometimes striped together. 1-2 ft.

NICOTIANA AFFINIS

Myosotis, Forget-me-nots.—In cool moist gardens these delightful little plants thrive and perpetuate themselves by seeds year after year. They are most admirable in early spring and may be used to underplant larger sorts or to make a brave early showing in beds and borders where later species are to flower.

NASTURTIUM, Tropœolum.—One of the richest and finest annual plants in cultivation and deservedly popular. All varieties may be grown in the border, though the dwarfs are best. The tall sorts are extremely well adapted to window boxes, lawn vases, and to situations where they may fall over rocks or down short slopes. The hybrids of Madame Gunter show many beautiful colors.

NICOTIANA, Flowering tobacco. The white fragrant *N. affinis,* is one of the really good garden annuals; but some of the hybrids are also excellent, though the colors need censoring. Some of the soft pinks are clear and safe, but the magentas are coarse and ugly. Best results are secured when the plants are started in the hotbed and transplanted to the border after all danger of frost has passed.

PANSY.—Known and admired of all. For small plantings buy plants of the florist in spring. To grow the plants sow the seed in the fall in cold frames, which are covered at the beginning of winter. Transplant from these early in spring. Or sow the seeds as early as possible in spring in the hotbed or in pots or boxes in the house. Buy good seed.

PETUNIA.—Very fine for heavy masses in the flower border. A solid block of petunias thirty or forty feet across gives a very striking effect, if not out of harmony with its surroundings. The free and easy luxuriance of growth and profusion of bloom cannot be surpassed by anything in the garden. Extra choice varieties may easily be grown from cuttings; but main dependence may be placed on seedlings grown in fall,

WHITE PANSIES IN A MIXED BORDER

winter or early spring, and transplanted to the open ground after all danger of frost is past.

PHLOX.—The annual *Phlox drummondi* is one of the finest border plants. Many people have become indifferent to it from having seen it so often grown in stiff, awkward flower beds. Such treatment takes all the grace and freedom out of the plant, which is inclined by nature to be a trifle stiff and serious. But when it is allowed to form free, irregular masses in the border, properly supported by other flowers, it is a very charming plant.

Poppy.—The annual poppies are very striking in color and graceful in form. They always seem at home in the mixed border, harmonizing with almost anything. The Shirley poppies are especially desirable, but there is hardly a variety grown which is not an acquisition.

Ricinus, Castor-oil bean.—These plants, of several different species, give grand summer effects. The varieties with dark foliage are especially beautiful. Should be started early.

Stocks.—Old favorites, but neglected in late years. Very useful in the border.

Sweet Pea.—One of the finest plants known for cut flowers and quite indispensable, but not well adapted to the hardy border. They are usually best put by themselves where they may have a trellis and good cultivation. They should be sown in the open ground at the earliest possible moment in the spring, or may even be sown in the fall. The selection of varieties is a matter of personal taste. There are several useful little manuals which the sweet pea lover should consult.

Verbena.—The low, prostrate habit of verbenas does not best suit them to mixed plantings in the natural method. A few of them may be used, however, in certain parts of the border, especially where the plantings come directly beside a footpath.

ZINNIA.—Well-known, old-fashioned flowers, but useful in many places. The newer varieties show some fine shades of color.

CHAPTER XXIII

THE BEST BULBS

No garden should be without a bed of bulbs. Beginning so early in the season,—weeks and weeks before the blooming period of the earliest annuals,—their brilliant and beautiful flowers are enjoyed more than those of summer.

E. E. Rexford.

Nothing can exceed the brilliancy and variety of color displayed by their flowers, and nothing can be more simple than their culture. *Mrs. Loudon.*

Along with the herbaceous perennials naturally come the hardy and half-hardy bulbous plants. They have in general the same requirements and the same capabilities as the herbaceous perennials. Many of them will live untended in the open border quite without protection, and thrive and blossom year after year. Some require winter protection, but all of those named here will last without replanting for several or many years.

It is to be noted that few or none of these plants are desirable for their foliage. They are all grown for the brilliancy of their blossoms. This requires that they be judiciously set to show against shrubs or such other foliage-covered plants as shall give them a suitable background. This is seldom taken into consideration. Lilies, gladioli and irises are almost always planted by themselves. They are left without support. They look lost and out of place. Anyone can see, as soon as it is mentioned, how much better they would look comfortably grouped with other plants.

The following list includes the best bulbous plants, with a few which do not grow from the bulbs, but which, in view of the use we make of them, may be best understood just here.

CHINODOXA, Glory of the Snow, one of the earliest and most delightful flowers of spring. Should be planted in a sheltered place with southern exposure in order to get the full value of its precocity.

CROCUSES.—Almost the first flowers of spring, and always welcome for their earliness and freshness. Where shrubs and herbaceous plants are grown in an open border, crocuses may be thickly planted in narrow rows along the extreme edge next the grass. One of the most satisfactory ways to grow crocuses is to scatter them thickly in the grass, where they will usually came up every spring without further care.

DAHLIA.—The dahlia is enjoying just now a well-deserved renewal of public favor. Many fine new varieties are being offered by the dealers, and great satisfaction is to be got out of their culture. The cactus varieties are the most informal and appeal more strongly than the older types to most tastes; but the single varieties and the smaller pompons, as well as the mammoth blossoms of the most regular outlines, have all their various agreeable expressions.

ERYTHRONIUM, Dog's-tooth violet.—These little

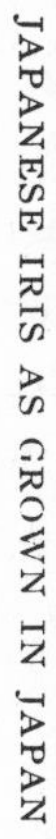

JAPANESE IRIS AS GROWN IN JAPAN

early flowering plants are very delicate and beautiful. There are several fine species and varieties, nearly all of which are hardy.

GLADIOLUS.—The gladiolus is one of the most striking and effective flowers in the garden when nicely grouped with other plants. When put by itself and with no company but an unpainted stick, it is one of the most awkward and ungainly sights on the lawn. The gladioli are especially useful for grouping in small masses among shrubs. They are also very valuable for cutting, and for this purpose may be grown in quantity in the reserve garden. There are hundreds of fine varieties, in many colors, but yellows and reds are best, especially reds. The bright reds and carmines seem to be the best suited to the character of the plants.

IRIS.—There are some fine, hardy, native irises, and a great many hardy and tender species of great beauty from all over the world which may be grown with a little care. The many varieties of German iris are all desirable, and the Japan irises are among the most gorgeous flowers ever seen in temperate climates. The Siberian irises are also very desirable for garden planting, while the more tender Spanish and English irises, (true bulbous species) are superlatively beautiful and may be grown with proper care.

LILY.—The noblest of flowering plants. Lilies should be scattered liberally in every flower border. They harmonize well with shrubs and herbaceous perennials, and the annuals may be mixed with them to great advantage. The following are a few of the best species for garden culture: *L. auratum,* Gold-banded Japan lily, one of the most popular and magnificent; flowers very large, white, banded with gold and spotted with red; requires replanting from time to time. *L. browni,* one of the finest, bears three to four flowers, seven to eight inches long, chocolate brown outside, pure white within. *L. canadense,* the common meadow lily, hardy, abundant bloomer, useful, in several shades of red and yellow. *L. elegans,* a very showy species, with large flowers in several shades of red and orange. *L. batemanniæ* is especially showy and fine. *L. grayi,* a fine, delicate, native species, small flowers, red. *L. hansoni,* a strong and beautiful yellow lily especially adapted to growing under shrubbery. *L. humboldti,* very strong and handsome, bears large orange-red flowers. *L. henryi,* not very cheap, but one of the most magnificent; should be planted by everyone who can afford it; flowers large, orange. *L. japonicum (Krameri,)* large flowers of a very delicate pink tint, quite unique. *L. longiflorum,* a fine, large, white lily. *L. candidum,* the common white lily, nearly hardy, a free bloomer and very attractive. *L. pardalinum,* flowers orange, with lighter center, a good sort. *L. regale* is somewhat new to American gardens but has achieved a considerable popularity, of very easy culture. *L. superbum,* a strong native species, bearing large numbers of red or orange blossoms. *L. speciosum,* one of the very best, especially the variety *rubrum.* *L. tenuifolium,* the Coral lily; somewhat dwarf, with many brilliant, coral-red blossoms; very desirable.

THE MADONNA LILY, LILIUM CANDIDUM

L. tigrinum, the well-known tiger lily; good. And there are many others. Most of these are better if covered in winter with a mulch.

LILY-OF-THE-VALLEY.—This old favorite grows best on the shady side of the house, or in a corner back of the porch, out of the sun. It is hardy and permanent wherever a spot can be found suited to its taste.

MONTBRETIA.—Looks something like a diminutive gladiolus, but is much more beautiful than such a description would suggest. Really a fine garden flower, hardy in California and the Gulf coast, and can readily be grown throughout the country by lifting the bulbs in winter as is the practice with gladiolus. Several good named varieties in various pleasing shades of red and yellow.

MUSCARI, Grape Hyacinths.—In various shades of blue, but all shades beautiful. One of the loveliest of all spring bulbs, and quite hardy and dependable. Indeed they frequently produce seed and come up self-sown in the grass or border. Plant them liberally along walks, in the edges of shrubberies and in the general mixed borders.

NARCISSUS.—This genus includes several plants of great usefulness in the hardy garden. The trumpet narcissi, often called daffodils, are especially fine, either in the general border or naturalized in the grass. Some of the best sorts for outdoor culture are Horsfieldi, Emperor, Empress, Bulbocodium, Poet narcissus, Trumpet Major and Incomparabilis. Narcissi can best be transplanted in June and July.

TUBEROSES may be planted in the flower garden or border with considerable satisfaction. They should be set in fall and covered with a mulch.

TULIPS make fine displays in early spring, and for a week the open bed in mid-lawn is almost bearable, so that we forget the manure heap which has been there all winter representing the necessary flower bed. But tulips may also be scattered in the border with other plants, or even set into the turf. There are many magnificent species and varieties listed and described in all catalogs. The best groups for garden planting are the cottage tulips, the Darwins and the varieties known as breeders.

SCILLA, Squills. These pretty blue flowers are amongst the first to greet the spring and as always welcome. They should occupy a sheltered border where the early sun will give them a prompt start.

YUCCA.—Nurserymen usually classify the yuccas with the bulbous plants, and perhaps they are as much at home here as anywhere. They must be used with caution, but in surroundings somewhat picturesque they may be introduced with fine effect. *Yucca filamentosa* is the species most generally used, but *Y. angustifolia* is also desirable.

CHAPTER XXIV

CLIMBERS

> Vines are valuable not only for their flowering effect but they are valuable for the effect of their fruit also. Some vines, such as the matrimony vine, with its brilliant orange fruit, the American bitter-sweet, with its red and orange fruit, together with the Virginia creeper, with its interesting blue fruit, are valuable in a landscape setting far into the winter months. *Albert D. Taylor.*

In making up a landscape picture proper, climbers are of minor importance. Their chief use, in purely naturalistic compositions, is not for climbing, but for trailing over rocks, or down sloping banks, or for clambering over low bushes. In such situations as these they are very effective.

But when buildings are introduced, and fences have to be dealt with, and unsightly objects need disguise or concealment, the climbers are indispensable. In the shading and adornment of porches they play no insignificant part in the list of the gardener's materials.

I wish to emphasize the fact that no climber ought to be planted on level ground unless there be first some suitable support on which it is to climb. It is not uncommon to find cases in which the climber was first planted, and afterward some crazy and impertinent structure was arranged to meet its demands. This is one of the ways of losing naturalness, along with all other kinds of beauty.

Wherever a permanent planting can be made, perennial climbing plants will usually be the more desirable. But for temporary and immediate effects, or to reinforce perennial climbers where they are too thin, or for window boxes, and similar purposes, the annual climbing plants are of great value. Some species of the latter may be started early in the house, and transplanted out of doors as soon as frost is past, so as to gain an earlier effect. The following brief list includes the most useful sorts.

WOODY PERENNIAL CLIMBERS

ACTINIDIA.—White flowers with purple centers. Still rare in this country, but destined to be popular.

AKEBIA QUINATA.—A dainty little climber from Japan, with small, five-parted leaves. Desirable where a large quantity of foliage is not required.

AMPELOPSIS.—The American ivy, Virginia Creeper, or Woodbine, *A. quinquefolia,* is one of the commonest, best and most widely useful of all climbers. The Japanese, or Boston ivy, *A. tricuspidata,* is excellent for covering stone or brick walls, particularly the latter. The Turquoise berry, *A. heterophylla,* is little known, but it is a very desirable species for general use.

ARISTOLOCHIA SIPHO, Dutchman's Pipe Vine.—A very hardy, vigorous climber, with large leaves. One of the best, especially in the northern states.

BIGNONIA, Trumpet creeper. A coarse, lusty vine

suitable for heavy duty and massive effects. The foliage is good and the flowers pretty.

CELASTRUS SCANDENS, Bittersweet.—One of the very best and hardiest climbers. To be recommended everywhere.

CLEMATIS, Virgin's Bower.—Several species and horticultural varieties of this group come up for consideration wherever climbers are wanted. The thrifty species with garlands of white flowers,—*C. paniculata, C. flammula, C. virginiana, C. montana,*—are the most useful. *C. jackmani* is always a favorite, for its large blue flowers, though it has nothing else to recommend it. Many other varieties bearing beautiful, showy flowers are to be had of the dealers.

ENGLISH IVY has many uses within its limited geographical range. The effects produced by its dull green foliage are altogether admirable.

EUONYMUS.—The varieties *E. radicans* and *vegetus* are excellent for growing against stone or brick walls. The latter is a stronger grower, with better foliage, and will usually be preferred.

FICUS PUMILA, the climbing fig, is a splendid species for use on brick or stone walls, or even on cement, in the region where it is sufficiently hardy, viz. Southern California, Louisiana and Florida.

GRAPE VINES of all sorts are excellent for landscape planting. The native American species are best of all, and of these the Fox grape, the Riverbank grape and the Summer grape are the best in the list, with a chance for Scuppernong is the southern states. Grapes are especially adapted to the planting of pergolas.

HYDRANGEA.—The climbing Hydrangea, *Schizophragma hydrangeoides,* though slow-growing, makes a splendid showing when once established. It is bet-

CLIMBING HYDRANGEA

ter than *Hydrangea petiolaris,* a similar plant with which it is often confused.

KUDZU VINE, *Pueraria thunbergiana,* is a most rampant grower and suitable for coarse work.

LONICERA, Honeysuckle.—Hall's honeysuckle, with its white or yellowish, very fragrant flowers is a favorite plant, especially southward, and is admirably adapted to covering rough banks. The old-fashioned climbing Trumpet honeysuckle, *L. sempervirens,* is very useful for neglected situations.

MENISPERMUM CANADENSE, *Moon-seed.*—A slender, twining plant which makes a nice addition to a collection.

ROSES.—The climbing hardy roses naturally come in for a liberal amount of attention in all planting schemes where climbers are required. Their foliage is good, unless it is bad. The trouble is that the foliage is often attacked by insects or mildew, and then the results are quite unpleasant. The flowers are, of course, the main attraction. The Rambler roses, in particular, are very great favorites, and may be successfully grown over a large part of the country. Other climbers, as the Memorial rose, the Cherokee rose, and some of the newer hybrids, may be planted in those restricted sections where they are known to succeed.

WISTERIA. A great favorite, and justly so, where it succeeds, but it does not succeed everywhere. In many localities it is quite shy in blooming; in some localities it almost never blossoms. This is a great disappointment, as its beautiful long trusses of pale blue flowers are greatly admired. Apparently it does better near the sea. Like most woody climbers it is slow in getting established, but makes up for all delay by enormous growth when once its roots have taken hold.

ANNUAL CLIMBERS

Balloon Vine.—An old-time favorite, to be found in all the old-fashioned gardens. The puffy, inflated seed vessels which appear throughout the summer are the most striking feature.

Echinocystis lobata, Climbing Cucumber.—A rapid-growing, luxuriant climber from the American woods, covered with garlands of white flowers throughout the season. One of the best for common planting.

Hop Vine.—One of the most rapid growing and useful climbers. It is one of the best annual plants for covering verandas or other large areas. The "Variegated-leaved Japan hop" is preferred by some, though the effect is not always good.

Maurandya.—Rather short climbers with abundant white, pink or violet-purple blossoms. Suited to more general use.

Mina.—A pretty and useful plant of the morning glory family, but with small flowers and lobed leaves.

Momoridica, Balsam Apple.—A favorite in old-fashioned gardens, and always good.

Morning Glory.—This glorious and old-fashioned climber has been too much neglected by modern amateur and professional gardeners. There are many magnificent new varieties now on the market, and they are so useful for many purposes that they ought to enjoy a new lease of public favor.

Sweet Pea.—The sweet pea needs no introduction

THE LUSTY, RAMPANT CUCUMBER VINE

or praise. In climbing over fences and low trellises it is thoroughly at home, while no known plant gives a finer harvest of flowers suitable for cutting.

TROPEOLUM, Nasturtium.—The climbing nasturtiums are extra fine for window boxes, lawn vases, and many other places. It is worth while, in planting nasturtiums, to choose the best-bred named varieties. The varieties known as Lobb's nasturtiums and the Madame Gunter hybrids are especially thrifty in growth and rich in gorgeous colors.

PART V

Bibliography

CHAPTER XXV

BOOKS ON LANDSCAPE GARDENING

And I, too, love my thatched cottage:
I have done my plowing;
I have sown my seed:
Again I have time to sit and read my books.

T'ao Ch'ien.

The literature of landscape gardening is extensive and delightful, but unevenly distributed. Some fields are well covered; others are well neglected. But any thoughtful student will find much that is worth his attention in books and magazines; and the collector who wishes to build up a library in this line will surely find a rich harvest awaiting him.

For the student or reader who is thoroughly enthused with the spirit of landscape study, and especially if one is studying the subject for the sake of his own personal pleasure in it rather than for the immediate good he may derive in planting shrubs, there is another considerable field of literature which he will do well to explore to the full extent of his opportunities. These are the essays and books which, under one name and another, deal with the beauties of rural life and are filled with the atmosphere of woods, lakes and mountains. Merely as examples of such we may remember John Burroughs (of whose books Winter Sunshine should be named first in this connection), the essays of Donald G. Mitchell (Ik. Marvel), the diaries of Thoreau, and the more recent nature essays of Dallas Lore Sharp, Liberty H. Bailey and many others. It would have been a pleasure to the writer to include a bibliography of these books in this chapter; but as that cannot be done, the reader will depend on librarians and book dealers who everywhere know and prize these books.

In the following much abridged list of books on landscape gardening only those are included which are of the most direct value to the beginner. It has been thought proper to omit those books, of which there are many good ones, which deal wisely with the naming and growing of different kinds of plants. By the time he has thoroughly studied these his horizon will have been so far enlarged that he can select his reading for himself better than anyone can do it for him.

AMHERST, ALICIA, History of Gardening in England, London, 1885. A very complete and satisfactory treatise on the subject.

ANDRÉ, EDOUARD, L'Art des Jardins, 1879. A French classic.

DOWNING, ANDREW JACKSON, Landscape Gardening, Original edition, New York, 1841. There are several editions of which the 6th is most famous and the 10th (N. Y., 1923) the most recent. A great American classic.

ELIOT, CHARLES W., Charles Eliot, Landscape

WILD PLUMS BLOSSOMING IN MAY

Architect, Boston, 1902. A touching and interesting personal memoir.

ELY, MRS. H. R. The Practical Flower Garden. N. Y. 1911.

GOTHEIN, MARIE LUISE, Geschichte der Gartenkunst, Jena, 1914, 2 vols., illus. Perhaps the best general history of landscape gardening yet produced.

GILPIN, WILLIAM, Observations on Picturesque Beauty, 1786. Also, Remarks on Forest Scenery. The latter especially is worth careful reading.

HUBBARD AND KIMBALL, An Introduction to the Study of Landscape Design, N. Y., 1917. One of the leading American works on the principles of landscape design by a well-known teacher and practitioner of the art.

JAEGER, H., Lehrbuch der Gartenkunst, 1877. One of the best German works on the subject. A good history of landscape gardening by the same author is entitled Gartenkunst and Gaerten, Sonst und Jetzt. 1885.

JEKYLL, GERTRUDE, Color in the Flower Garden. London, 1908. The standard work on color.

KELLAWAY, HERBERT J., How to Lay out Suburban Home Grounds, N. Y., 1915.

KING, MRS. F. The Well-considered Garden. N. Y., 1915.

LANGE, WILLY, Gartengestaltung der Neuzeit, first edition Leipzig, 1906; several subsequent editions. One of the most thoughtful and constructive of modern works in the entire field of landscape gardening.

MIGGE, LEBERECHT, Die Gartenkultur des 20. Jahrhunderts, Jena, 1913. Ills. A brief but illuminating statement of conditions and principles, with special reference to Germany.

MILLER, WILHELM, What England can Teach Us about Gardening. N. Y., 1911. A book of dashing criticism illuminating many of our American problems.

NICHOLS, ROSE STANDISH, English Pleasure Gardens, N. Y., 1902. A delightful and useful work, especially in its historical aspects.

PARSONS, SAMUEL, Landscape Gardening, N. Y., 1891.

——— How to Plant the Home Grounds, N. Y., 1899.

——— The Art of Landscape Architecture, N. Y., 1915.

PRICE, SIR UVEDALE, An Essay on the Picturesque as Compared with the Sublime and the Beautiful, and on the Use of Studying Pictures for the Purpose of Improving Real Landscape, 1794. This is published in many editions. The best one (*fide* Mrs. Van Rensselaer) is that of 1842, edited by Sir Thomas Dick Lauder.

PUCKLER-MUSKAU, PRINCE HERMAN L. H. VON, Thoughts on Landscape Gardening. A famous German work appearing first in 1834. There are various editions, but the most accessible is the American translation by Bernhard Sickert published in Boston in 1917.

REHMANN, E. The Small Place, N. Y., 1918.

——— Garden Making, Boston, 1926.

REPTON, HUMPHREY, Observations on the Theory and Practice of Landscape Gardening. Many editions dating back to 1803. The most available is the American edition of 1907 edited by John Nolen and published in Boston. A famous English work by one of the greatest of English landscape gardeners.

ROOT, R. R. AND KELLEY, C. F. Design in Landscape Gardening, N. Y., 1914.

ROBINSON, WILLIAM, The English Flower Garden, 1883. There are several editions of this fine work. The later ones have been revised by the author, and a great deal of descriptive and illustrative matter added. Describes and illustrates large numbers of plants.

SIMONDS, O. C., Landscape Gardening, N. Y., 1920. A leading American landscape gardener gives his mature views on the main matters.

TAYLOR, ALBERT D., The Complete Garden, N. Y., 1921. Mainly devoted to plant lists elaborately analyzed with reference to the needs of differing localities and types of gardening.

TRIGGS, H. INIGO, The Art of Gardening, a historical sketch. London, 1913.

UNDERWOOD, LORING, The Garden and its Accessories, Boston, 1907. A useful work dealing with garden furniture and accessories.

VAN RENSSELAER, MRS. SCHUYLER, Art Out of Doors, New York, 1893. A most delightful book dealing with the art, not with the practice, of gardening.

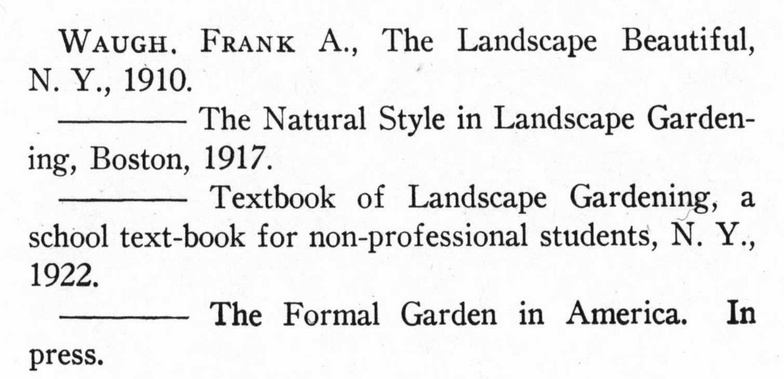

WAUGH. FRANK A., The Landscape Beautiful, N. Y., 1910.

——— The Natural Style in Landscape Gardening, Boston, 1917.

——— Textbook of Landscape Gardening, a school text-book for non-professional students, N. Y., 1922.

——— The Formal Garden in America. In press.

INDEX